A Mental Attitude to Dressage

A Mental Attitude to Dressage

LÉONIE M.
MARSHALL

J. A. Allen
London

British Library Cataloguing in Publication Data
A catalogue record for this book is available from the British Library

ISBN 0.85131.739.1

Published in Great Britain in 1998 by
J. A. Allen and Company Limited,
1 Lower Grosvenor Place, Buckingham Palace Road,
London SW1W OEL

Typeset by Textype Typesetters, Cambridge
Printed by Dah Hua Printing Press Co., Hong Kong

Design by Judy Linard

Contents

Introduction

Why should anyone want to ride dressage? I have wondered this frequently myself over the years! Personally I came into dressage by default, having acquired a new horse who was greatly opposed to jumping! Once I 'had a go', however, I was instantly captivated and soon realised why others found the subject so absorbing. Training a horse to the top levels is an exciting challenge which tests a rider's skill to the utmost.

In dressage today there is a minority of riders who enjoy training their horse for training's sake and do not wish to be competitive, but there are many more who look on it purely as a competitive sport.

Not that many years ago, in Britain anyway, the term 'dressage' was a dirty word, but now the pendulum has swung the other way and almost everybody trains their horse on the flat, and huge numbers compete. With an ever-increasing number and range of classes being organised anyone and everyone can take part in some competition if they so wish.

Although this is an excellent state of affairs for the health of this branch of riding, it is questionable whether it is really such a good idea for the individual unless the material is suitable and the rider has the right mental attitude. There is nothing more frustrating than trying to catch hold of something just out of reach. Whether the barrier be physical or mental, there are times when it is necessary to concede to the impossible. Although I would be the first to advocate the benefits of dressage training for every horse, I do believe that each individual should question their own motives and abilities before embarking on what is, after all, a very serious and involved form of equestrianism.

Anyone who follows dressage accepts, I am sure, that it is ultimately an art, but as only a small number of geniuses are born, this zenith of attainment is reached by only a few. What is not so generally understood is the high degree of brainwork required, as well as the necessity for consistent physical effort. To any art there is a proportion of science attached; for example, the painter or sculptor must know anatomy and must also be able to plan out certain subjects geometrically. Very few people succeed at anything without a lot of study and forethought, backed by logical and detailed planning. This has then to be followed by dedication to a daily routine.

In dressage, making a decision on the level of ambition requires reference to the potential of the horse, if his well-being and the rider's contentment are not to be compromised. Much therefore depends on the mental (as well as physical) aptitude of the individual – and this applies to both horse and rider! Those who wish to reach the top will require a positive attitude, as it is all too easy to be discouraged. Anyone doubtful of their ability to 'stick at it', or who simply does not have the desire to train on a daily basis, might be wise to consider exploring other alternatives.

Having determined that dressage competitions are the aim, the rider should accept the need to learn how his mind works; how physical responses, voluntary or involuntary, relate to his thoughts and in what way this contributes to failure or success.

Those who compete already are fully aware of the 'buzz' that accompanies the arrival of the new Omnibus schedule! The adrenalin starts to pump long before the coffee is made and the schedules studied; now, however is the moment of realism! Whether the goal is modest or magnificent, each person should assess their own capacity to succeed. Having done so, the classes should be chosen carefully according to the training, which should be to a higher level than the class entered.

The planning having been done and the responsibilities understood, the rider has put himself into a position to tackle the project, and must tell himself to 'go for it'!

1
Biology and Psychology

Taking part in competition is a demanding business and, without sufficient knowledge of the way our own, and our horses' minds and bodies work, it may be impossible to assess or analyse performance in way which is crucial to a satisfactory result.

As the emphasis of this book is on mental rather than physical aspects, I do not propose to discuss biomechanics, except to remind readers that, with the best will in the world, a rider will not be able to force himself to operate beyond the limits of his physical ability.

Although all actions are governed by the mind, a rider's build and ability inevitably influence the way in which the horse goes, which is reason enough to understand fully one's functions and limitations.

The Nervous System

In the world of sport, performance is much affected by state of mind. Those competitors who can stay cool under pressure are fortunate indeed. There are many more who suffer consistently from 'nerves'. Control of 'nerves' requires training and willpower, so in order to learn how this may be achieved it is necessary to have an idea of the function of the nervous system.

The system is responsible for many things, such as control transmission, co-ordination of nerve impulses, regulation of respiration, heart rate, digestion and emotions: all the things, in fact, that can particularly affect anyone taking part in a competitive event.

While all parts of the nervous system are inter-related, they are all under control of the central nervous system, which contains the majority of the body's neurons (nerves). The peripheral system connects the nerves of the brain and spinal cord to other parts of the body; the somatic system transmits information such as pain, pressure or temperature from the skin, muscles and joints to the central system; and the autonomic system regulates respiration, heart rate and digestion, and also plays a major role in emotion.

NEURONS

The human brain is made up of a network of specialised nerve cells (neurons) which are the base units of the nervous system. There are three types of neurons:

Sensory neurons transmit impulses from the skin, joints and muscles and detect physical or chemical changes in the body.

Motor neurons carry outgoing signals from the brain or spinal cord to muscles and glands, where they initiate action.

Inter-neurons receive signals from sensory neurons and send impulses to other inter-neurons or to motor neurons.

The relevance of this knowledge to the average person is chiefly to enable them to recognise or interpret signals that the body gives, in order to know what to expect.

HORMONES

Many bodily reactions result from actions of the various glands connected to the autonomic system; glands that secrete hormones which determine an individual's level of energy, mood and ability to cope with stress. Although our control over hormonal influence may be limited, we can to some extent take control over the stomach constriction or increased heart rate that being 'keyed up' produces. Also, while it is important to performance to keep the adrenalin pumping, it is equally necessary to train the mind to be calm, so that inhibiting tensions can be released.

RELAXATION AND MENTAL CONTROL

Without the right level of relaxation, the mind and body cannot operate fluently. One of the paths towards achieving this entails learning to breathe properly. Tension often induces shallow breathing, which prevents the necessary intake of oxygen and reduces the necessary exhalation of carbon dioxide. Breathing correctly controls the level of adrenalin produced, thus calming the body. However, there is something of a chicken-and-egg situation in that correct breathing requires a level of relaxation, or a conscious desire to achieve it. With modern stresses and strains, recognising this need is an art in itself. However, it is an asset in any walk of life, and is worthy of some study. Apart from books on the subject there are also tapes to listen to and, while the advice given may have to be adapted to a riding situation, it can nevertheless be very helpful.

Aside from physical relaxation, control of 'nerves' is aided by focusing the mind on something specific; in the case of a dressage competition it will be on the way in which the horse is going, and on the test. The focus needs to be absolute so that all distractions remain outside the core of concentration. This takes experience, and can only be developed with determination and practice.

Knowing what may cause the mind to send out panic signals and cause bodily reactions we do not want is also helpful. Most people who compete panic for a variety of reasons. One common one is that they are afraid they will make fools of themselves; another is that they may let down their teacher or their family. Many people worry that they will forget the test, or ride badly on the day. All such fears can cause the body to react in ways that hinder or destroy what we hope to accomplish. Only by learning about ourselves can we hope to train our minds and bodies in such a way that our actions can be planned and controlled.

Physical fitness

I have already talked about the question of correct breathing in connection with relaxation and the need to supply oxygen to the body, but its relationship to fitness is equally important.

It seems that there are some dressage riders who do not fully appreciate how fit they need to be, and this is particularly relevant at the higher levels where longer tests are ridden. Fatigue, or lack of breath, will obviously hinder performance, as anyone who has had to sit for long periods on a big-moving horse knows well! However, the accent is often more on getting the horse fit than the person who is going to do the riding! Naturally, fitness is crucial to both horse and rider, in order that undue strains are not inflicted.

RIDING TOWARDS FITNESS

There are many ways to get fit and each individual will have his own preference. There are choices such as aerobics, swimming, running or 'working out' in a gymnasium to name a few, but there is no doubt in my mind that the best way to become 'riding fit' is by riding – while the horse develops in muscle and strength, so does the rider. Of course, 'riding' can take various forms and those who merely amble about without a clear programme will not progress very fast! Just as the horse needs to be worked methodically, so does the rider. A plan of action must be formulated which encourages the right development of mind and body and this can only be done if the rider provides himself with adequate knowledge of what he wants to achieve, and how it will be done.

Development of bodily muscle and strength can only come about from the rider sitting correctly on the horse and learning to apply the aids effectively. The right saddle for the job is essential to the rider, to place him in the right position and to help him maintain it. Thus, appropriate muscles will be made to work as the rider adapts to the contours and movement of the horse. Also, as the rider's seat develops, signals sent to the horse will become co-ordinated in such a way that they can be made clear and consistent.

Many people, of course, come into dressage from other spheres where muscle development has been suited to their particular purpose. Adaptation will be necessary, but it can only take place gradually; to expect a quick result is a mistake and will only lead to frustration. Although the 'experts' make dressage look easy this is part of their skill; it is in fact very hard work! Only by a routine build-up does a rider become fit enough for the action ahead.

HEALTHY EATING

This brings me to my next point, which is the matter of inner health and the digestive system. On this subject I am bound to bring up that unpopular word – diet!

There is little doubt in my mind that the ultimate dressage picture is of a slim, elegant rider on a beautiful horse! Unfortunately, it must be accepted that the 'ultimate' generally eludes us, but in order that horse and rider have the best chance, whatever their aim, control of weight is important.

When working with horses it is all too easy to rush to 'convenience' food, or to 'snack' at intervals, both of which are unsatisfactory to digestion. Furthermore, many snack foods are full of calories! I am only too well aware of the feeling of deprivation (and sometimes mental anguish) that being on a diet can cause! There are two things which I have found personally helpful; one is to alter one's thought pattern and the other is to keep an account of the calorie intake.

Changing thought patterns takes quite a bit of doing, as each person has developed their own ideas regarding what they eat and drink over many years. It is a matter of re-training the mind to accept what is the right amount and type of food to take. This does require some research, but it basically involves avoiding too much fat or sugar. This can be calculated with the aid of a calorie book, and by monitoring what is purchased and what it contains. This sounds a bore, but it is surprising how quickly it is possible to learn. What does take longer is training the mind to enjoy what is suitable!

Many people find calorie-counting too irksome a task but it has one big advantage over some other methods. This is that no substance is actually forbidden, so long as it is included in the daily count. If you simply cannot walk past the chocolate counter, the baker's, or the chip shop you can succumb, so long as this is not done too often. This is where a change of thought is needed, so that the mind is distracted by some other activity.

Determining how many calories an individual may take in one day is dependent on such things as height, age, any medical problems, and the work being done, but with some trial and error, and the aid of some good scales, the right amount for either losing or maintaining weight can be discovered.

Much human behaviour relates to the need for food and drink and also to the physical state of the body. Obviously, the better we look after ourselves the more positive we feel – and the better our performance.

Learning

Physical aspects apart, success can only be achieved from the right knowledge and the ability to put it into practice. As we know, the human brain is a remarkable machine which, given the right information, can store it in the memory and recall it when desired. It is clearly essential to give it all necessary facts so that, once sufficient knowledge has been stored, all relevant details can be 'computed' and recalled simultaneously. However, during the learning process, there will inevitably be 'time delays' in recall. We should be aware of this possibility in order that our expectations of a particular reaction do not result in frustration when it fails to materialise.

Learning to co-ordinate mind and body takes time and practice and, as this process also has to be 'married' to the horse, who has his own problems, no-one should expect to achieve it without work.

ENVIRONMENT

Environment is important factor in learning. At school, we are placed in a situation where the brain can absorb what it is given, and where it is being worked consistently each day. After leaving this environment, the mind becomes exposed to dozens of other aspects of life, which all need their own space. This often means that our riding has to be fitted in between other things and, if time is limited, this can present problems.

There is no doubt that, in order to be successful, time must be given to mental preparation before even getting on the horse! Only by doing this, and then being somewhere peaceful away from everyday distractions, is it possible to lean and apply what is necessary.

Although families often encroach, or business thoughts invade the mind, it is important to develop the art of concentration so that outside influences are restricted.

STUDY AND PRACTICE

If the subject of dressage is new – or even if it is not – a certain amount of research into it is advisable. Every sport has its rules which have to be studied. There are also different methods to be analysed, and a great deal to learn about what precisely is expected. There are various ways in which this may be done, such as reading books or magazines, watching videos, listening to audio tapes and so on.

Of course, however much knowledge is acquired, theory is nothing without practice. Instruction is a good way to build up 'know-how' but it is important, if possible, to go to a reputable trainer or judge, who is, or has been, a competitor. Unless this is done the art of 'ring riding' may not be discovered. At first, dressage riding may appear mystifying, but a good teacher should be able to show how a systematic and logical approach will produce results.

MOTIVATION

Everyone has their own faculty for learning, and it is easy to be discouraged by apparent limitations. However, with sufficient thirst for discovery and enough studying, it will be found that there are few barriers to progress. Thus motivation will play its part in determining success; those with a strong will to do well will advance more quickly than those who are lukewarm. Therefore, everyone would be well advised to question their own motives for wanting to ride dressage. It may be an undeniable compulsion that provides that inner drive but, if the desire is too superficial, the secrets of learning may not be discovered. The real enthusiast will want to know everything possible, whereas those who only use their horse to further their own ends will never reach the heights.

2
Mental Affinity and Horse Sense

Instinctive Behaviour

Knowledge of the horse; his needs and anxieties, will undoubtedly help us to comprehend his responses. To do this it is important to know how the horse lives in the wild, as this awareness enables us to see why he behaves as he does.

The most dominant instinct is the need to survive, which provides natural exercise in the search for food and water. This necessity is still uppermost in the horse's mind, as is also an acute awareness of those enemies in his distant past who skulked behind bushes or dropped from trees. Although he may be protected by domesticity, these instincts hold firm, with most horses still basically motivated by fear and flight and many equine responses being rooted in these reactions.

In order to form a satisfactory rapport and working partnership we need to understand our horses' fears. No training will be really successful without this knowledge. Providing reassurance is imperative in training as, without being calm, our horses cannot function well. We must also learn about our own fears and what these may cause us to do. Just as the horse is governed by his natural instincts, man's sense of self-preservation causes many involuntary reactions. Any action that is not calculated may be disruptive to the aim, therefore we need to know and understand what causes us to react as we do.

Our main fear is probably that of being hurt; of falling off and breaking something, so we quite often react simply for our own protection, without due thought for our horse. In such a situation the horse himself is reacting according to his own instincts, but this is when conflict and misunderstanding can occur. The action taken at such a moment can either improve the matter or make it worse! We also suffer from the fear that we shall look silly or let ourselves down. In these circumstances our dealings with the horse may be either ineffectual or heavy-handed.

When riding dressage there is often a fear of forgetting the test, but it is important to realise that any indecision on our part will be felt by the horse.

HORSE SENSE

It is often said that a person either has, or does not have, 'horse sense' and although this is very true it is not easily explained. The best way I can describe it is that those who have it possess an intuitive knowledge of how their horse will react, with an instinctive ability to respond in the right way. It might be reasonable to assume that experience and learning about horses would give a person 'horse sense' but, while I am sure this applies to some extent, I believe that true affinity is really a gift. In dressage, such a natural affinity is obviously a boon, as the closer the horse and rider are to each other, in every way, the better their performance.

In many cases of course, 'horse sense' consists largely of placing oneself and one's horse in a position to achieve a successful outcome, rather than one that courts disaster! It is all too easy after the event to blame the horse when, with more forethought, the problem would not have arisen.

Sensitivity and Rapport

Those people who have true empathy with their horse will treat him as a partner, working through difficulties with him, rather than being in opposition. Of course, there will be occasions when there is a clash of minds, in which case the successful trainer will have to use ingenuity to work out a satisfactory conclusion.

Trust and patience will go a long way towards winning the horse round to the right way of thinking, but this will only be developed if the horse is treated with respect. Just as real 'horse sense' eludes some people, so does the quality of sensitivity. Unfortunately, it is not easily learned, but it is another area where determination can aid success.

Being a tactful communicator with a sympathetic approach is a good start. Make friends with the horse in the stable, for there you gain the first stage of respect that will be so important once training starts.

Provided that the horse is taught how to behave on the ground, learning by a method of correction and reward, he will respond to his trainer in the right way when ridden. Although he will have much to learn, the horse will have already accepted basic control. Once a basis of understanding is established, the horse's natural inclinations will take a back seat as he listens to his trainer. Obviously, the trainer must have sound knowledge so that all instructions are given in a way that the horse will comprehend. Also, it is crucial that the trainer recognises whether the instructions have been carried out correctly.

Any alterations or improvements to training should be done tactfully but firmly, the degree of firmness being determined by the circumstances and the stage of training, and by the temperament of the horse. All corrections should be followed by praise, either with the voice, or by giving the horse a pat on the neck.

The Senses

In both horse and man the senses trigger the response to every stimulus. All responses to stimuli will be affected by past experiences but, if no such experience is stored, the response will be purely instinctive. It is not feasible to put the senses in any order of priority, since all are crucial and they often interact with each other. However, since it is necessary to start somewhere, I will begin with the sense of sight.

SIGHT

Function

Since the basis of sight is the same in humans and horses, with some small differences, I shall discuss it in general terms.

Each sense organ responds to a particular type of physical energy, in this case light. Light enters the eye through the cornea, which is regulated by the diameter of the pupil; the lens then focuses the light on the retina. The lens focuses images of objects, at various distances from the subject, while the pupil controls the degree of light required for this operation.

Colour Vision

Whereas man has the advantage of seeing images in colour the horse is less fortunate. Although it is not proven that horses cannot see in colour, research has indicated that it is most likely that they are only able to distinguish shades of dark or light. Although, in training, it may seem that the horse reacts to some strong colour, he is probably merely seeing a more sharply defined shade of dark. If his reaction is fear of the object, this could simply be related to instinctive fear of shadows where predators lurked in times past.

So far as we are concerned, it is the case that some brightly coloured objects will instantly catch our attention. If, by our own anticipation of trouble, we transmit negative messages to the horse, he will follow suit and look for trouble himself.

Shapes and Patterns

From our own experiences of life we are able to rationalise our fears and we learn to distinguish those objects which may be of danger to us. The horse, on the other hand, is more likely to have to rely upon images or patterns and, depending on how these are projected on his mind, he will react accordingly. So often in training it seems that the horse has a dislike of a particular object, sometimes to the point of stupidity. It is necessary to understand that, if that object has caused the horse to fear it at any time in his life, or if he relates it to some similar experience, the image in his memory may cause a negative reaction.

Giving reassurance is one of the trainer's main tasks, and this will be easier if one is aware of what the horse may be thinking. Of course a situation may arise in which the horse reacts badly because of some past experience of which the current owner is unaware. If this should occur it is important to overcome it, as otherwise the anxiety felt by the horse could develop into a phobia. Some horses take a lot of convincing but only by tackling the situation firmly and calmly can it be dealt with.

Because the question of identifying images or patterns may cause the horse concern, it is clearly of great importance to introduce any object in the right way. As many strange objects will be presented to the horse – especially in new situations – the wise trainer will prepare for this by introducing as many of them as possible at home first. There will, of course, be many things to consider, not all of which can be replicated. A common hazard is that of dealing with strips of sunlight on the ground, reflected through windows or perspex sheeting on the roof of an indoor school. Some horses will naturally try to hop over or skirt around them. Only by encouraging confidence in the rider and instilling obedience can this be overcome. Similarly, riding out of light into darkness or vice versa can bring problems until the eye has had time to adjust. Every trainer should know about this and make allowances.

Blindness

There is ample evidence that this handicap will not prevent determined people from riding and competing in dressage. In fact many do seem to have a sixth sense, obtaining a 'feel' for the size of the arena, sides of an indoor school and movements to be ridden. If they have hearing, then guidance may be given from the ground, and this is often necessary.

So far as the horse is concerned, total blindness is an irrevocable handicap and should be easily recognised. Partial blindness, however, is a different matter and does not necessarily mean an end to the horse's career. It may be hard to discover in the first instance, as it is not until something happens to provide a clue to the possibility that a diagnosis can be made by a veterinary surgeon. It must be said, of course, that a horse with sight in only one eye may have problems (especially of straightness) which demand great patience on the part of the trainer.

HEARING

Function

Whereas the eyes are sensitive to electromagnetic energy, the ear responds to mechanical energy; pressure changes in the atmosphere, such as vibrations, which cause compression or expansion in the air molecules. The consequent sound waves are the stimulus for hearing. They are received by the external ear and conveyed by the auditory canal to the eardrum. Each individual may respond to pitch or loudness in different ways, depending on their capacity.

Capacity

It is generally thought that the horse's hearing is more acute than our own. He certainly has one advantage in that his ability to rotate his ears allows sound to be picked up very quickly. So often, in training, the horse seems to hear something of which we are unaware, causing him to lose concentration. It is easy to be irritated by seemingly irrational behaviour, but this should be avoided since any tension may damage the bond which is being built up.

Reaction

As with sight, past experience will cause certain reactions. For instance, a loud or harsh noise may be associated with a 'telling off', whereas softer sounds have a soothing effect. In this context it is clearly important to the horse that his trainer's voice should be used in such a way that the intention is plain. Consistency is the way to teach the horse, who will soon learn when he is to wake up, or to calm down.

Sound waves can cause a sudden reaction if they come unexpectedly, having the effect of making us 'jump'. The horse reacts in a similar way if he is startled and, if his response takes us by surprise, our normal reactions may be affected. In any situation where there is loss of control, momentary or otherwise, confusion may follow.

There is also the matter of complex sounds, which are several noises jumbled together. In such cases the horse may lose concentration and the rider may lose co-ordination and train of thought. Identification of sounds can delay the required responses. As riders we must be prepared to control our own reactions and to give reassurance to the horse if necessary.

Familiarisation with New Sounds

To avoid disruption of training, new noises should be introduced singly if possible, and also gradually. The playing of a radio with music and voices is a good plan, plus any other noises that are likely to occur at a competition. Of course, it is not possible to cover every eventuality. Cattle breathing heavily on the far side of a hedge; the sound of carriage wheels; the Household Cavalry, harness clanking; aircraft landing; these are hazards that even the most diligent trainer cannot foresee! In such circumstances training may be severely tested, and the hazard surmounted only if there is a real bond of trust.

Deafness

Deaf people are not hindered in any way from competing successfully – other than that they may fail to hear the starting signal! In this case it is wise to have a helper who can indicate when it has gone. Of course, if the rider loses the way there can be a problem in hearing the judge's signal, so it may be sensible to have the steward advise the judge beforehand in order that an alternative arrangement can be made.

I have never known a deaf horse, although I have known plenty who give that impression! I am not aware of any consequential training problems and assume that horses do not suffer from this particular disability except, perhaps, in old age.

SMELL

Function

From an evolutionary viewpoint, smell is one of the most primitive of the senses. It has a more direct route to the brain than any other, and it is intended to guide behaviour. Sensitivity varies a good deal with different species, dogs being especially high on the list. Horses, like most animals, rely on their sense of smell for identification and communication. From secreted chemicals known as pheromones they can attract other members of their species and identify gender.

Signals

Pheromones constantly convey signals relating to other members of the species, either encouraging them to approach or warning otherwise. For instance, a mare in season may or may not give off encouraging signals depending on the time of her cycle. One stallion approaching another will receive warning signals other than smell, but will know from the pheromones whether to keep his distance. Riders also give off signals to the horse, although these are unwittingly given and are generally involuntary. For example, any nervousness or sweating will be detected as, of course, will a female rider's monthly cycle.

Where signals are especially strong the result is often for the horse to lose concentration, which can cause problems in training. One of the lessons the horse has to learn is to listen to his trainer's instructions, regardless of other influences.

Identification

To the horse, the identification of the things he smells is crucial to him in determining their potential danger. He will identify things by investigation, possibly touching as well as sniffing the object in question. If he is prevented from following this method of identification he may easily become upset. If he is allowed to draw his own conclusions he will either dismiss whatever it is or decide it is a danger to him. If he concludes the latter, his reaction will probably be flight. So long as the rider is aware of this possibility he will be forewarned and can act accordingly. Even the best-trained horse, however, may present his rider with problems if some sudden primeval fear overrides normal behaviour.

Out of his home environment the horse will encounter many unusual smells. It will be up to the rider to give him as much reassurance as possible.

TASTE

So far as the dressage rider is concerned, sense of taste is irrelevant – except perhaps for the sometimes bitter taste of defeat! The horse, on the other hand, will respond to certain tasty bribes during training. In my experience, these should not be offered too frequently while the horse is being ridden, but should be used as a reward at the end of a training session. This will give him something to look forward to, and helps to cement the relationship.

Some trainers like to reward the horse with a titbit following acceptance of a difficult exercise. The only danger in following this method is that the horse may be looking for a reward, which can be distracting to him and may disrupt the flow of work.

TOUCH

The familiar sense of touch includes at least four skin sensations that may be associated with riding. These are pressure, pain, heat and cold.

Function
The precise receptors for the various skin sensations have been the subject of much research and two things can be stated with some certainty. First, the nerve fibres at the base of the hair follicles serve as receptors for light pressure, but they are not the only receptors since the lips – which of course are hairless – are also quite sensitive. Second, free nerve endings that end in the epidermis are involved in pain reception.

Pressure
In all dressage riding, the application of pressure by the contact of the rider's legs and by the hand via the reins to the horse's mouth, is essential to control. One of the chief aims of training is to teach the horse to respond to the lightest pressure (aids) possible.

During training, however, the horse must learn to accept firm aids, as only by giving these at times will the trainer communicate his requirements. Firmness should, however, be used in such a way that resentment is avoided so far as is practically possible.

The use of aids and applied pressure will be discussed later, but it is worth remembering that a response can only be expected if aids are used on those areas where the skin receptors are most sensitive and easily stimulated. These areas are the horse's mouth and around his girth.

Pain
The second of the skin sensations is actual pain. For the horse there are three main sources of pain; that which is inflicted intentionally by the trainer, that which is caused unintentionally through ignorance or lack of sensitivity, and that which is caused by some physical problem.

Intentional pain. In training, the application of pressure alone may sometimes be insufficient to alert the horse to his rider's intention, therefore a follow-up use of a whip may be necessary. Of itself, the whip is a harmless item in the horse's terms, unless he associates it with some degree of pain. It is necessary to ensure that the horse does answer the whip when it is used, and that he is respectful of it. Individuals vary a great deal in their response to a whip, chiefly because some have a more sensitive skin than others. Determining how to use a whip to gain a result will obviously depend on the response made. A trainer will soon get to know an individual horse and use the whip accordingly.

It is important for the horse that he fully understands the reason for pain applied, and that he is always rewarded for the right response to it. Failure on the trainer's part to recognise the response will cause confusion in the horse's mind and will place the partnership in jeopardy.

Unintentional pain. There are occasions when, because of human failing, the horse is reprimanded insensitively or out of context. If the trainer does not take himself in hand, the horse may lose confidence in him or become opposed to work in general. There may also be times when, because of a sudden or unexpected reaction by the horse, the rider is caught out. At this time the horse's mouth or back may suffer from the rider losing balance or becoming annoyed. Horses are so frequently blamed for their riders' own ineptitude! It is in these situations that the horse will look for ways of saving himself from pain; thus are evasions born!

Physical problems. The third source of pain is physical injury or lameness, both of which can cause great distress – particularly if the problem is not recognised or, worse, ignored!

It is amazing how thoughtless supposedly caring owners can be. A sore back or chronic lameness, lack of proper care of the feet, or injuries caused by tack may not only prevent a horse from doing his work, but will surely make him resent it also. It is strange that some riders seem oblivious to their horse's distress, while others simply appear not to care. These are two remarks that have been made to me many times, either when teaching or judging:

'Oh! He is putting on his lameness to get out of work'.

'Oh! He is always like it'.

What foolish and insensitive comments.

Reaction To Pain

Temperament plays quite a large part in the different ways horses react to pain. The more highly strung they are, the more obvious or violent the reaction may be. Thoroughbreds (though not all) come into this category, as most have sensitive skins with little hair covering. Those with a 'laid back' outlook and thick coats will take a lot more rousing.

Reactions to any pain felt will be chiefly from the sensitive areas of the mouth and girth region. It is easy to understand that the bit can cause terrible pain if used badly and that the horse will avoid this by throwing up his head, overbending, or opening his mouth – to name but a few responses. If a rider is unaware of the damage he may be doing, and continues to cause harm, the horse's mouth will gradually become less sensitive, thus making control more difficult.

So far as the girth area is concerned, although sensitive receptors are located there, this does not mean that there will be an automatic response. Discovering this fact may tempt the rider to resort mistakenly to the use of spurs as a pain-inducing incentive. In this he could be disappointed, since only if the horse is already aware of the meaning of leg aids will he be receptive to the spur. In addition, any persistent use (especially if uninformed), may serve only to deaden sensitivity.

Heat

The sensitivity of skin to temperature changes can cause harm unless the horse's owner is aware of them. The main occasions when overheating could pose a problem are during travelling, when being worked, or if the weather is particularly hot or stuffy.

So far as travelling is concerned, it is clearly necessary to adjust clothing according to the prevailing heat, which may perhaps be influenced by the number of horses travelling together. When travelling by road, the horse may sweat up because of the efforts of keeping his balance and also if he becomes anxious as a result of being driven or 'cornered' too fast.

Transporting horses by air or sea requires common sense. For example, the hold of a ship is exceedingly hot, so light clothing may be best for the horse.

Travelling is often a traumatic or claustrophobic affair for the horse and he cannot be expected to do his best if he arrives at a show 'in a state'.

Natural sweating during work is normal, provided that it is not caused by anxiety. Sweat on the neck or between the back legs shows that the horse has been 'working'. One point to look out for, though, is sweating on one side of the neck only, as this would indicate uneven use of muscles.

It is always important to allow a 'cooling off' period after work and never to rug up a sweating horse and leave him unattended. Where a competition is held in very hot or dry conditions it is vital that the horse has plenty to drink (at appropriate times). The use of electolytes to replace lost body fluid may be necessary, since dehydration is very dangerous.

Cold

Dressage training requires a horse to be fit, but he will only be up to the job if he is fed properly, which helps to keep him warm, and rugged and bandaged sensibly. Any sudden drop in temperature may mean providing extra warmth. A cold horse will quickly shiver off his condition and shivering also puts muscles under continuous strain.

In winter it may be necessary to avoid loss of condition from sweating but, having taken away the coat, extra warmth should be provided. Many horses find clipping a frightening experience. It is up to each owner to tackle the job with tact.

3
Character and Temperament

There is little doubt that being a successful competitor requires not merely good training, but also individual determination and an ability to divorce oneself from all outward distractions.

Traits of character and temperament are determined by a continuous interaction between heredity and environment. Our genes decide many of our characteristics; skin and hair colour, general body size, gender and, to an extent, our intellectual ability and emotional temperament. Experiences from birth onward interact with our genetic make-up and go towards determining our development.

These factors apply not only to humans, but to horses as well, although equine make-up is less complex than human, and the horse is unable to express himself in human emotional terms.

In humans, character traits provide certain ingredients which make them potentially strong competitors, or otherwise, depending on what the traits are. For instance, a person endowed with good levels of activity, concentration and confidence, will have an advantage over one who is prone to apprehension, self-consciousness or over-sensitivity under stress. Also, those who are open-minded and adaptable will be more successful than those who are too arrogant to change their views.

Clearly, a positive attitude very much affects performance in the arena, but the element of past experience is also a major factor.

Controlling Emotions

In all training an individual's empathy with the horse, and an ability to put theory into practice are key factors, but even with natural gifts, much hard work is necessary in order to gain control over inevitable human reactions.

Whatever a person's basic character or temperament, reactions under stress may not be completely controllable at the time, but it is important that a quick recovery is made. Recovery time will vary, partly depending upon temperament, but also on how the mind has been trained.

Not everyone is blessed with patience so, in certain situations, it is natural to become agitated or despairing, particularly when a new exercise is being learned. Not only does the rider suffer from feelings of frustration at his own apparent inadequacy but the horse, too, may well be confused and anxious. It is easy to understand how impatience or anger distorts reactions, thus making aids become muddled. Controlling these reactions is another matter. In the main, a sound knowledge of what the aim is and how to arrive at it reduces the possibility of becoming stressed, but it must be said that, even with this knowledge, the frustrated 'artist', aiming for perfection, may not be able to prevent the occasional outburst! (Of course, despair is not the only emotion felt in training – there are also moments of joy.)

Our reactions to our own emotions are clearly perceived by the horse and, according to his own temperament, these feelings may be complemented or otherwise. For instance, the anxious type will not complement a rider who becomes excitable or nervous under stress; alternatively, a horse of bold nature may react to anger by becoming aggressive himself. It is clear, therefore, that a full understanding of our own responses is just as important as understanding those of the horse.

Training a horse requires a bond of mutual trust and respect added to which, from the human angle, there may be the element of 'love'. Most horse owners, I am sure, would profess to 'love' – or be very fond of – the horse they are training. Without some affection the partnership would perhaps even fail. This sentiment must, however, be put into perspective as regards training because of the need for discipline. Sometimes it is not easy, or even very nice, to make the sort of demand necessary, but those who find it hard – even unacceptable – must realise that their training progress will be very limited.

The old saying that a horse cannot be trained without blood, sweat and tears is well known. In fact, tears are so often a useful outlet for extreme disappointment! There is nothing wrong with this, and most successful people alternate between ecstasy and misery! Dealing with disappointment is not easy, but it is important to remember that the horse does not experience such feelings and may not understand his rider's reactions, which may vary from aggressive to pathetic! To those who react badly when disappointed I would give this advice: get off the horse as quickly as possible before you do something you might be sorry about, and remember that a damaged partnership is never quite the same afterwards.

Of course, disappointment and failure are generally only temporary, so there is no need to become depressed. What is more important is to review what went wrong and to make a firm decision about future plans.

Not everyone who rides and competes is bold; many are actually quite nervous. This can be a handicap in competition, especially if combined with 'ring nerves' as well. Quaking knees or tighter than usual rein tension are indications to the horse that something untoward is going on. This may happen even if the rider is not a nervous type, but if there is actual apprehension about being thrown off, or getting out of control, then this is a problem indeed. In a situation such as this I would advise further experience at home before venturing out again. Dressage is a very demanding sport, needing a positive attitude and firm riding ability, and it has no room for weakness of any kind.

Determination

The possession of an iron will is one of those indefinable qualities which those who have it recognise, and those without it cannot understand. No-one else can provide you with a will to win; it is an uncontrollable inner compulsion that drives the body and lends power to the mind.

Being a dressage rider certainly demands a strong will in order to overcome human weakness and channel the natural will of the horse from pleasing himself to pleasing the rider. With such determination comes the dedication to stick to a daily routine and to follow it religiously. From time to time a rider's resolve may be dented, but a fundamental will to win will bring him back on course.

Horses, of course, are sometimes as determined as their riders to have their own way. While they do not have the same interest in winning, they may just be as strong-willed in pursuit of their own ends. This is just one of the hazards of training, and much depends on how the mental strength of one partner is handled by the other. Being compatible is important but strength of character, whether it be human or equine, should command respect as, harnessed in the right way, it becomes a valuable attribute.

Confidence

Confidence in competition is arrived at in three main ways:

1. Having the ability yourself.
2. Knowing that the horse has the ability.
3. From the knowledge that preparatory work has been well done.

Let us consider each of these points in turn:

Riding ability. It is pretty plain that if there is a lack of empathy or 'feel', this can be a serious handicap to the aspiring dressage rider. However hard he works, and however determined he may be, he will know inwardly that he has limitations, whereas the rider with natural flair will have inner confidence.

Ability of the horse. Owning a horse with the physical ability to go 'all the way', who instantly catches the judge's eye, is a tremendous confidence-giver. Less able horses give the rider a sneaking feeling of being 'up against it', even though he may not want to admit it.

Good training. This provides the best basis for confidence. Knowing exactly what is wanted is the first step, followed by diligent attention to detail so that there are no flaws likely to interfere with performance. It is all too easy to be over-ambitious too soon, but there is nothing more dispiriting than knowing in your heart that you have not really put in the necessary work.

There are at least two things which can interfere with the build-up of confidence. These are problems arising from being over-confident and a 'show-off', and indulging in self-doubt.

The over-confident often ride with insufficient thought for their horses, and tend to over-react to mistakes by impatience or insensitivity. Pricked pride can make us behave in an obnoxious way that offends others and causes the horse distress (since he usually takes the blame!). Over-confident people are also often bigoted in their opinions, refusing to alter training methods even when advised by people more expert than themselves!

Although this state of affairs does not encourage progress, neither does the rather negative attitude of some who are so lacking in confidence that their self-doubt completely blocks any advancement.

Neither arrogance nor too much humility have a place in training; an open mind, combined with an unswerving desire to do well, are more suitable ingredients.

Of course pride in your work is necessary, so long as it is not misplaced, and criticism can still be accepted. A reasonable degree of confidence should provide the competitor with a cool head and clear thought. It will not encompass the sort of dominance over the horse that produces robotic performances, but should enable the rider to co-ordinate mind and body in such a way that his influence over the horse results in a harmonious performance.

It is very easy to lose confidence, either as a result of a disappointing performance, or in the light of some criticism by a judge or other person. In the face of criticism it is all too easy to become over-sensitive but it is important to remember that, without critical appraisal of your work – whether by judges or yourself – not much progress will be made. Accepting criticism without becoming dispirited is all part of the job. The best thing to do is to sift the constructive from anything destructive and go on from there.

Mental strength is, of course, a big help as its effect on a rider is that it provides positive action to which the horse can respond. If this makes him bolder in his work he will be more likely to give of his best. Passive riding, on the other hand, will not help the horse and opens the door for a moderate outcome.

By using accepted training methods and progressing steadily over time, the development necessary for a true partnership can evolve. From this sound base horse and rider build trust in each other, so that each has the confidence to do their best.

Assessing the Horse

When starting out with your chosen animal, it is all too easy to be under the happy illusion that the natural skill and determination you possess will carry you through. This is a most unwise belief which is very likely to be dashed in the first outing!

There are several points to consider with regard to the horse. These are: his conformation; his action; his size; his age; his temperament and also, most importantly, his 'star quality'!

Although, logically, correct build should provide the horse with the ability to operate well, it is surprising how often this rule proves to be false. Nevertheless, I would personally prefer to produce a horse with the best conformation possible, provided that other suitable ingredients are there.

Good action is essential because, if there are any limitations, regardless of how good the training is, there will be may movements affected. In particular, if it is not possible to differentiate between the variations of gait, this will restrict the marks.

Generally speaking, the horse's size should pretty much 'match' that of the rider. There are obviously problems in having a horse who is too small for the rider but, however talented the rider, it will always be relatively harder for them to ride a horse who is significantly too big than one who is a 'good fit'. Since successful dressage demands the finest nuances of control, compatibility of size can be an important consideration.

The same thing, essentially, applies to the question of age: the horse's age and experience should match as closely as possible the aspirations of the rider. In particular, do not buy a young, inexperienced horse if you are impatient to compete at the higher levels.

An equable temperament that can take the rigours of training is essential and should, if at all possible, be determined prior to purchase. The importance of a good temperament; one that is as unflappable as possible and also willing to oblige, cannot be emphasised enough. Riding on a knife edge can prove very stressful under competition conditions, but the sort of horse who will let you 'ride for your life' is a great confidence-giver.

To define 'star quality' is virtually impossible, as it is an elusive quality that is not easily recognised. It is based, I believe, on fundamentally good gaits combined with scope and spring, good conformation, and spirit. A horse with 'star quality' stands out in a crowd, being able, in his own way, to project personality as well as looking the part.

Discipline

Winning cannot be achieved without discipline, of both the horse, to obtain the necessary obedience, and of oneself, to ensure that the right routine and procedures are followed. It is hard to drive oneself and equally hard sometimes to accept discipline from others. It is all too easy to blame a 'weak leg' or 'bad back' for poor riding quality; bad weather or illness are much-used excuses for not keeping up with training.

Horses also find discipline a trial, especially if they are strong-willed. Learning how to extract the right responses without crushing spirit is quite difficult, but both humans and equines can accept correction if the reason for it is made clear and the required alternative action is properly indicated.

Because dressage is such an exact sport, firm control over mind and body must be observed – and this applies to both partners. Only by diligently following classical training methods will flaws be eradicated and a steady rise in standard achieved.

Daily routine can be drudgery and many are put off by this aspect of training. It is a fact, though, that the routine is necessary, so it must be accepted if winning is the aim. Finding the necessary motivation is sometimes hard, but anyone with enough inner compulsion will overcome this.

4
Riding Ability

There is little doubt that an individual's natural ability, or lack of it, plays a big part in their attitude to training and ring riding – particularly with regard to confidence. Other matters of relevance are: physique; 'feel'; co-ordination; the ability to communicate, and concentration.

Physique

Although, generally speaking, a person's physique does not prevent them from becoming a top rider, some are embarrassed or self-conscious about their shortcomings, and this may affect their whole outlook and approach to training and competing, especially since any self-consciousness in the arena will destroy confidence and positive thought.

The variations of human build present advantages and disadvantages to the individual concerned. It is generally accepted that the ideal build for riding dressage is to be tall and slim. Certainly, clothes look well on this type of individual and give an elegant appearance that suits the job. This gives the slim rider the advantage of confidence in the way he looks – which is one less thing to worry about!

Even so, long legs can bring about problems, especially if they extend below the horse's belly. Maintaining contact and being effective can be frustratingly difficult. In such cases it is worth remembering that the aid effect must be acquired from the lower leg as a whole, not from the heels.

Short stature also has disadvantages as there is less leg to wrap round the horse, and it can also affect the size of the animal suitable for that rider.

Being overweight probably causes a rider more embarrassment than anything else. Not only is it far more difficult for an overweight rider to keep close to the horse, and maintain the right influence, but clothes are often uncomfortable or stretched to the limit!

Since self-esteem is so important in the arena and any psychological distraction, such as worry over appearance, is a great hindrance, it is essential that everything possible should be done in the preparation at home to overcome such thoughts.

Whatever an individual's build, it is important to attain good deportment, and this must be part of the discipline of the daily routine. This is essential, not only to the right presentation but in order that the influence of seat and other aids is maximised. Stiffness and tension caused by mental frustration or anxiety are two of the biggest inhibiting factors in riding. Development of a good position, well maintained, is vital to success and, whatever a person's physique, this will entail hard work – nothing is easy!

Choice of the right horse for each individual's shape and size is also crucial, as is the right equipment, especially the saddle, which must fit and be comfortable for the rider as well as the horse. Once these points have been established it is up to each rider to take a positive attitude.

Feel

This word is used to describe a rider's intuitive response to his horse's actions, which unites horse and rider in a harmonious manner. To some it is a natural gift; others have to strive for it!

For both rider and horse, balance is the biggest criterion. Those who can instantly feel when it is lost will be able to regain it more quickly. In fact, talented riders will be aware even before the event, thus preventing a problem, or at least covering it up quickly. When watching competitors in the arena, it is easy to see those who keep their horse balanced through their own natural feel and those who, because their own balance and feel are lacking, are constantly struggling.

Of course, it is possible to learn to develop feel. A good 'schoolmaster' can help in this respect. Anyone lucky enough to ride or own one will progress as a result of the experience. However, it should be remembered that any 'schoolmaster', although mentally retaining his work, will gradually become physically 'rusty' if not kept up to the mark by an experienced trainer. Furthermore, although riding a 'schoolmaster' teaches the feel of various exercises, it does not provide the rider with the feel of the various stages of progression which occur during training. These can only be learnt by training a horse from the start.

The right rapport with the horse will help in identifying reasons for his actions, thus helping mind and body to respond accordingly. This rapport is achieved through relaxation and suppleness, which allows the rider to bond closely to the horse, and provides the opportunity for both to concentrate on each other.

Without the development of feel the rider will not find the ultimate harmony that he seeks, and will thus limit his goals.

Co-ordination

The close linkage between mind and body is essential to a rider's ability to apply aids comprehensively and effectively. Talented riders are blessed with natural co-ordination which, for them, happens without a lot of planning or thought. Lack of this talent often results in a disjointed performance, which frustrates the rider and is unpleasant for the horse. Frustration causes so many training problems and frequently compounds itself as one irritation piles onto the next.

Acquiring good co-ordination of aids, and so reducing the chance of causing or aggravating problems, is not a simple matter. It requires much mental discipline and concentration. Thus training is not only physically demanding, but mentally very testing as well. The way aids are given is absolutely crucial to the whole outcome; they must therefore be totally clear in the mind of the rider and executed efficiently. This often takes some planning. First, the mind must be prepared, then it must instruct the limbs to carry out the thought. For some, this process is well-linked; for others extra preparation may be needed.

Much thought should be given to how messages are sent to the horse, as only if these are given well can he be expected to respond in the right way. Certainly the hasty use of aids is bound to cause difficulties, and so is any tension in the mind or body.

Maintaining the right sort of contact with the legs and hands is absolutely essential, and this entails constant thought about what each is doing in relation to the other. Furthermore, these aids cannot be applied well unless the seat is secure, so this is also a vital matter.

It is a fact that feel and co-ordination go together and cannot exist without each other, but unless the rider is mentally confident, his body will not act as it should.

Communication

The rider's natural aids: voice, seat, legs and hands, are the chief means of telling the horse what is required of him. These aids must be used in a co-ordinated way (in simultaneous or almost simultaneous combinations) so that messages are clear. Any physical action is, of course, initiated by the brain, and this must possess the necessary knowledge in order to send appropriate instructions. I would like to emphasise this point as I see many novice riders who are physically unable to express their intentions to the horse because of their lack of knowledge. The concept that dressage is simply aiming the horse from A to B, without control of each step, is not going to get anyone very far!

Satisfactory communication can only take place if the rider had planned clearly what he wants to do, tells his horse, and then gives time for the answer. In other words, good preparation is essential. Without it there will be loss of balance and subsequent resistance. Therefore a study of how aids are to be given, combined with consistency and plenty of practice, is clearly essential.

The Aids

THE VOICE

This aid is the horse's first experience of human communication. He will soon learn that it can convey praise or disapproval. It expresses what the trainer is thinking and is therefore most important to his future work.

The voice is used as a training aid, first in the stable to teach the horse how to behave, then on the lunge or long reins to teach words of command, and finally under saddle where all previous orders must then be related to other aids, so that these can become the chief influence of control.

In the dressage arena use of the voice is penalised since, by the time the horse is ready to compete, he should be so prepared by having been taught the seat, leg and hand aids that the voice is no longer a requisite. Having said this, in practice many riders (especially those with novice horses) still use the voice in the arena – although if it is overheard it will receive a penalty.

The clever trainer will develop various vocal sounds which the horse understands such as a 'click' to increase energy or a brief 'shush' to set off an extension. Softer sounds may be used to reassure an anxious horse. Although all this may be 'against the rules' my belief is that a young horse should be helped along in his training at all costs, so long as the ultimate aim is not forgotten.

In training at home it has been my experience as a teacher

that many riders completely undervalue their voice as an aid, and simply do not realise how much better a response they could get if it were used more often, especially for praise. The voice, combined with a pat on the horse's neck, is the main means of letting the animal know he has done what is wanted.It should never be underestimated.

THE SEAT

I have already mentioned the need to sit well; to be balanced and supple. This factor is important in any discipline but especially so in dressage, where the horse is trained to respond to small differences in weight distribution.

Any looseness in the saddle or lack of close contact will weaken the aids, and may well upset the rider's original intention. This can only result in confusion.

Crookedness of the seat is a big fault, since aids will be uneven and, not only will the horse have difficulty in complying with them, but he will almost certainly become crooked himself.

Much mental anguish could be avoided if time was given to the correct development of the seat from the beginning. Work on the lunge on a good horse with a knowledgeable trainer is certainly an excellent way to start.

LEGS

Combined with the seat, the leg aids are the next most important means of communication. Unless the horse is taught to understand their meaning early in his life, he will develop his own ideas and may be reluctant to change these at a later stage.

If the rider sits as he should, the inside of the thighs will rest flat to the saddle, enabling the lower legs to wrap round the horse. This brings the whole leg in as close contact with the horse as possible. This is essential in order to be effective.

The position of the lower leg is determined by the stirrup leather being vertical to the ground. The rider's heels should be lower than the toes, but not forced down into an unnatural or tense position. The toes should never be turned out, as this draws the leg away from the horse, thus preventing the necessary contact.

At the start of training, the horse is taught by a combined use of the rider's voice, leg aids and schooling whip, the latter being a necessary reinforcement to the legs, which mean nothing to the horse at this stage. Once the horse has understood the association between the legs and the whip its use can be reduced, although it should still be carried in case it is needed.

Some riders are reluctant to use a whip, but this is a misguided attitude. The object is to train the horse to answer the lightest aid possible, and this is achieved with the help of a whip.

Knowledgeable trainers may use spurs, but this is not advisable for the less experienced as much damage can be done if they are used incorrectly. Spurs do become compulsory dress from Medium Level onwards, but they are intended to 'fine tune' a performance and should not be used to force a reluctant horse to work.

One of the most psychologically destructive factors in dressage is if the horse 'switches off' in the arena. Some do become crafty but, in general, the fault lies in inadequate discipline in obtaining the right answer to leg aids at home.

HANDS

Although all action is controlled by the mind, the hands reflect a rider's lack of thought or sensitivity more than any other aid. They are responsible for so many of the faults seen in training and competition. Faults such as horses not going forward enough, resistances to the bit, stiffness and woodenness, leaning on the hands, unlevelness, loss of rhythm – and I could go on!

These results of poor communication by the hands are rooted in several issues. They may spring partly from lack of natural balance and ability, partly from lack of knowledge, and frequently from insufficient forethought.

One point crucial to the whole matter is that of being

able to take and keep the right kind of contact. This is perhaps the most puzzling of all the aid applications for the rider to determine. If the rider keeps too little contact, the horse will not be sufficiently aware he is being asked anything; if it is too strong he will feel too restricted to respond positively.

Resolving these problems is not simple, and they cannot be easily dealt with in abstract. Real solutions will only be discovered through practice. In the first place, the horse must go forwards so that there is energy to control. Then he must necessarily 'yield' to the bit – if he does not, all contact will be dead! The rider should seek to establish the kind of contact that is elastic but fairly firm, indicating that impulsion is taking the horse forwards. This elasticity can only be discovered by the rider developing a 'feel and ease' action with his fingers; allowing energy forwards but regulating its degree.

At all times the horse's balance should indicate to the rider whether or not his influence is correct. If it is not, the hands alone cannot be the improving factor. This must come from the seat and legs that engage the horse's hindquarters, thus enabling him to propel himself in a balanced way. Only then do the hands have their part to play in the distribution of energy. This engagement must be done with careful thought as to the degree of energy required at that time for a particular movement then, through the sensitivity of the hands, the horse is 'allowed' to perform it.

It is all too easy to interfere with or actually prevent the horse's response by having too much or too little tension on his mouth. It is important to remember that the hands are there to 'talk' to the horse, not to carry him!

In this respect the search for self-carriage should be paramount, as only from this will a performance become easy.

Concentration

No competitor will be successful unless he possesses, or trains himself to have, the power to focus his mind totally.

This power shuts out all outside activity, preventing him from hearing or seeing anything which might be distracting.

Much of this skill develops from mental training which directs the mind to focus on how the horse is going. This level of concentration develops by long hours of practice and is associated with a gradual emergence of unity between horse and rider. This unity bonds the two entities mentally as well as physically.

Of course, it is not easy to overcome lapses in concentration; the rider needs to have a whole-hearted desire to succeed, and to be completely absorbed in the task at hand. It is only normal for mistakes to occur during a performance, and when they happen they can seep perniciously through the barriers of concentration. The disciplined rider will not allow this to go so far that he disintegrates under pressure, but will be able to bring his mind back quickly on what is to come, not dwell on what is past.

TRAINING AND HOMEWORK

Given the level of strain a rider is under in competition, it is necessary to have the advantage of laying down a sound foundation of training.

Getting on with the trainer is most important, as progress will be limited if there is friction. Although the trainer chosen should be superior in knowledge and experience, if temperaments clash there is no future on either side. To obtain the best from a trainer it is essential to believe in him, trust him and do as he says. If 'homework' is done diligently, progress will be obvious to both rider and trainer and, as a result, each will develop faith in the other.

As a teacher I have found that most pupils wish to please and to show how they have improved. Sometimes they are disappointed as things go wrong simply because they are making too much effort. Teachers understand this, as they themselves have struggled in the same way. The confidence they can give in such circumstances should encourage the pupil to carry on. No-one needs to despair if results do not come as quickly as desired. Even very minor improvements are well worthwhile.

It is sometimes necessary to go backwards in order to go forwards again! This can be frustrating and upsetting but, if the goal is to be reached, it must be expected and accepted as part of training.

Practice and Experience

In all competitive spheres, sooner or later it becomes necessary to test yourself against others. Only by such comparison will your true level be apparent. At home everything can seem to be going well, but this state of affairs can be altered dramatically by the disturbance of a show. It can be unnerving to leave the safety of one's own small pool and jump into a fast-flowing river, but only by having such courage will a competitor gain experience to survive and stay afloat.

Of course, progress should be well planned and must of necessity be gradual, so that the horse is not asked to face something new before he is ready. The rider, also, must be mentally prepared for taking steps into unknown territory in order that he can cope with any eventuality.

LEARNING FROM MISTAKES

Learning from mistakes is an inevitable feature of competition. Sometimes a mistake can take you by surprise, at other times it is a result of doing something foolish because you have given the matter too little thought.

No-one enjoys unpleasant experiences, but they are bound to occur. When they do it is important to learn from them so that they are not repeated. Determination is the key; those riders with little or no resolution will sink and disappear in the face of too much effort, while others will square up to the struggle and put it into perspective.

WHEN TO COMPETE

One of the problems the competitor has to deal with is

knowing how often to go out to compete. On the one hand, the more classes entered the greater the experience, giving the rider plenty of practice to develop technique. However, this can be a retrograde move if problems arising cannot be dealt with because there is too little time between shows to make improvements. Staying at home is often hard, but it may be necessary to sort out a difficulty or bring training a step further on so that the horse is better prepared.

Making the decision is often best done in consultation with the trainer, who can advise on the frequency and levels of test to be ridden. Ambition is the driving factor behind all competition, but it can serve to make us want success in too much of a hurry. The wise competitor will remember the saying 'make haste slowly'; a very apt remark in the context of dressage.

LEARNING TESTS

At first sight a printed test sheet can be exceedingly daunting, especially if a good memory is not your best feature! It is surprising, though, that once an initial group of letters and probable patterns is taken in, learning tests becomes relatively easy. It is getting started that can be hard. There are several ways of doing this.

First, it can be done by tracing the test out on a sheet of paper and drawing the movements over several times. Alternatively, some people mark out a small area in their garden and actually walk through the tests. Another useful way to learn is to sit behind the marker at a competition, where the whole test can be watched from the rider's viewpoint. Of course, riding a test several times makes an impression on the mind. The only snag is that it also makes an impression on the horse, who then soon anticipates the movements! If all else fails you can, of course, sit down somewhere peaceful and simply learn it! On the subject of a peaceful environment one way of learning tests that I found useful was by going over them just before going to sleep at night. They seemed to come back readily in the morning.

In the lower level tests there are relatively few movements and very often these are placed symmetrically – the movements on one rein being 'mirrored' on the other. This sort of test produces a pattern easily recalled. Other tests are not symmetrical but, once the mind is trained, a memory sequence is established which can often anticipate the movements most likely to follow each other. Make sure, however, that you check your 'guesses', so that you do not programme your mind to remember a sequence which is actually incorrect. Remember, also, that tests of the same level can be very similar, and this can be confusing. When riding two such tests it is important to expel the first test ridden from one's mind and to bring the next to the forefront. Standing by the arena repeating to yourself where each new movement starts is helpful in achieving this. When entering the arena it is a good idea to remind yourself which way you are going to turn at C, as this often triggers correct recollection.

When 'commanders' are allowed they can, of course, be utilised to good advantage, especially if several tests are to be ridden on one day. However, they should never be considered as a real substitute for memory. In FEI tests and championships commanders are not permitted, so it is essential to have taught yourself to remember tests, and this is best done by starting at the lowest level and working your way up.

One other point about learning tests is that, within every movement, there may be some specific detail regarding reinforcement of a particular aid which it is also necessary to remember. In training it is not possible to obtain the exact answer every time, and the horse may be less established in certain areas – which is why such reinforcements are necessary. The successful competitor will be able to focus his mind upon the way that his horse is performing as well as on the test itself.

DAILY ANALYSIS

Planning work to be done each day is very important as is analysing whether this work is taking training in the right direction. This analysis should be made each evening so that the mind is clear about what is to be done the next day. It is not always easy to find the time to do this. Often business or personal matters get in the way, but if time is not made it is easy to get in a muddle. I know well the feeling of arriving in the school and then thinking: 'What shall I do?' This vague attitude cannot produce anything worthwhile.

Dressage is essentially about gradual development, which only comes about from routinely and consistently ridden exercises. This, of course, involves a certain repetition but it should not be boring. It is important to plan what you want to do, otherwise you may find yourself riding 20 m circles for half an hour!

At each training level, certain new exercises are introduced. As these are attempted each may require special concentration until fully grasped, but once this is done they must be incorporated into the general training. It is very important that each exercise is considered not as a separate entity, but as part of a scheme that builds the whole. So long as all the basic principles are present the rider should give the horse as much variety in his work as possible.

Every school movement demands its own degree of elasticity and energy. The rider should acquire the knowledge to know whether he has made it possible for the horse to fulfil his requests. He will discover this by trial and error and with help from his trainer. Although some problems need an experienced eye, others can be thought through in a logical manner. Riders can help themselves a good deal in this respect by the application of logic when assessing their day's work. It is so often a question of cause and effect, and with due concentration on the cause, an answer can be found.

There are many causes for errors in training. Common ones are:

1. The gaits are not correct.

2. The horse is unbalanced.
3. The horse is not straight.
4. The horse is not 'on the aids'.
5. Preparation was insufficient.
6. Knowledge of the exercise was too limited.
7. Horse or rider lacked concentration or were distracted.
8. The tack was uncomfortable.
9. The horse was unfit for the work he was being asked to do.
10. The horse was over-fresh and therefore not receptive.

These faults are more easily corrected if they are properly identified, and this means taking time to think about them.

Also it is useful to interpret the signals that the horse give us. Such signals may include:

Resistance to the bit: pulling; leaning; tilting the head; putting out the tongue, etc. The rider's hands or the bit may be the cause.

Worried look in the eyes. This can tell us a lot about our training. Trust is all-important.

Ears back or flicking nervously. The horse either dislikes his work or is apprehensive about it.

Plunging, bucking or rearing. Lessons have not been made clear or established. Too much pressure too soon contributes to such problems.

Kicking to the aids. The horse has not been taught to accept the rider's leg aids in the proper manner, or they may be given unsympathetically.

Napping, whether passive (refusing to move) or active. The rider has failed to teach the horse to accept his requests and has allowed him to become the boss!

These signals by the horse tell us of his confusion or distress. Training can only be successful if the rider understands, is sympathetic, and aims to develop a mutual bond.

PLANNING AHEAD

From knowledge accumulated by the means laid down in this chapter it should be possible to formulate some plan for the future. Whether the aim is to ride in the Grand Prix or not, every rider should have some idea of at least a yearly aim, which will provide him with a month-to-month stage plan. This may entail listing the events at which you hope to compete.

Knowing what the aim is for the year will help when considering what work will need to be done in order that it may be achieved. If the same logic is applied to a monthly and weekly plan, the daily routine may become more obvious.

Plans, of course, can go wrong and it would be foolish to stick rigidly to them regardless of circumstances. Even if a daily plan is decided upon, it may have to be abandoned if the horse is not responding as he should. There can be so many reasons for this, but the point is that all forward planning is just a rough sketch, and detail can only be filled in when the moment is right.

5
Accumulating Knowledge

For all of us the process of learning starts at a young age and gathers momentum through the teenage years, culminating in final examinations on various subjects at different levels depending on whether we have average, or above average, mental ability. This process lays a foundation for the future and, while many of us subsequently discard the use of that type of brain power, it is nevertheless latent within us, waiting to be reactivated at a later date in our lives, if we so choose.

In order to become a successful dressage rider, active use of the brain is essential and the serious student must be prepared to use his intelligence to the maximum. There are many ways in which a student may further his riding knowledge and, although trainers and teachers of all kinds may contribute, it is up to the student himself to extract what he needs to know from many sources.

Most is us learn to ride in a riding school, and our first few years are often spent using the sport more as an amusing hobby than a serious subject. At some point, however, a person's ambition is sparked off, generally as a result of a particular experience such as seeing a display, or suchlike. At this point the serious rider will want to learn how to advance his ability towards the direction he has chosen – in our case, competition dressage.

Because riding can be nothing without practice, there is frequently more accent upon the practical aspect, rather than the theoretical. Dressage riders, however, must accept that understanding the theory of their chosen sport is of equal importance to actually doing it.

Instruction

There are many ways of increasing knowledge, the most obvious being that of obtaining instruction from a dressage expert. Very few dressage riders 'get there' without a good teacher, whether they have lessons on a regular basis or at less frequent intervals. Continental Europe is well endowed with trainers with years of experience behind them and many riders do take advantage of this fact. If it is impractical to consult such people, work at home must be done with the help of someone who has ring experience, and who has the knowledge to help train horses of different types and temperaments. He should be willing to impart this knowledge and help pupils to overcome their own difficulties wherever possible.

Riding through a problem yourself is one of the most valuable lessons and, although there may be times when it is necessary for the trainer to ride the horse, you will not learn much if he gets on every time there is trouble. My experience has been that too much reliance on a trainer detracts from the process of discovery which is necessary to build knowledge and feel. Also, if the horse becomes too accustomed to his trainer, he may be at a loss under this own rider.

Further to this, I would stress the point that, although it is a teacher's job to impart knowledge, he is not there to provide the pupils with motivation. This, they should have for themselves, as a result of their own ambition. It is, on the other hand, reasonable to expect the teacher to provide inspiration by giving an insight into what is possible.

Help, then, is essential, and it is readily available. It is up to every rider to choose how frequently to seek it, while also learning as much as possible from their own experience.

The main value of taking lessons is to find out the aims,

and how to reach them, and then to be diligent in doing the 'homework', so that real progress can be made. Only by so doing will a higher standard be attained and the goal eventually reached.

'Schoolmasters'

The value of riding a 'schoolmaster' in order to learn to feel the movements has already been mentioned. Certainly, if the 'schoolmaster' has not become too stiff through age, and is still able to move in a supple way, he can be very useful. However, although it is important for the less experienced rider to learn what aids to use and how to give them, unless his seat is really secure he will gain little, being unable to sit into the horse. A good 'schoolmaster' is a powerful ride, so anyone with a weak seat will be quite unable to sit strongly enough, and once the horse becomes 'disengaged', he will not give the right feel. Furthermore, it is important to realise that any attempt to alter such a horse in any way is unwise, and that it is best to learn to ride him as he is.

Riding a 'schoolmaster' can be exciting, useful experience, but does not teach a rider how to reach that end result. This must be done by training a horse oneself.

Reading

To back up this basic groundwork, the serious dressage rider must be prepared to study books on the subject in order to understand the aims, methods and techniques used. This should go on 'hand-in-glove' with the daily physical experience, so that each is related to the other, with the theory used as a check-up.

At first, the student should aim to read material set out in the simplest terms possible, since it is all too easy to be put off by long passages of technical jargon. At a later date, in the pursuit of higher knowledge, greater detail will be required.

Readers will find that there is some variance to training methods, depending on the author's nationality. Sometimes this is confusing until sufficient knowledge is gained to allow you to determine what could be relevant to you and your particular horse. It should be remembered that, although there are basic principles of training with a combined aim, each horse and rider are individuals – so there can be and often are different ways to arrive at that aim.

Lecture/Demonstrations

Many people take in a visual explanation more readily than a written one, although the picture still has to be backed up by theoretical study. Therefore, a useful way of finding out about the various methods of training is to go to lectures or demonstrations, where explanations of the methods are given, followed by their execution.

Much depends on the lecturer's charisma as to whether the demonstration will inspire, but if it does it will help, not only to further knowledge, but also to promote interest and provide determination to succeed. It is also a good opportunity to ask questions about training, but bear in mind that no trainer can give specific answers unless he has seen the horse in question.

One of the most important points to remember when attending a demonstration is to go with an open mind. The object is to learn, even if things are going wrong. There will always be some useful hint or point to be stored in the memory for a future occasion.

If you are ever asked to give a lecture yourself you will find that the research needed to do so effectively is immensely stimulating. There is, of course, an art to lecturing: apart from the actual content – which is vital – the way it is delivered is also important, in order that your audience does not drop off to sleep!

Videos

There are many videos available nowadays and these can be of tremendous help to the aspiring dressage rider. On the whole the quality of camera work is good, but beware; any slight fuzziness will distort the picture so that the eye may be deceived over the purity of performance. This applies also to home videos, which are invaluable to training as a personal check-up. Many a fault can be spotted by replaying the tape, although sometimes this can be soul-destroying!

It is important to remember that a video is a training aid. Do not be put off if, at first, you cannot stand the sight of yourself! Persevere and watch the improvement. (I must make the point here that some people watch themselves on film but do not improve as they should. It is not pleasant to accept faults or criticism but, if a video is taken of a test, do study it carefully in conjunction with the judge's comments and try to see his point of view.)

Watching Experts – and Others!

One of the most useful ways to learn is by going to a competition to see how others do it. Much can be discovered by observing the techniques used by the top riders, but it can also be useful to spot faults being made by the less knowledgeable.

Seeing the ways experts ride tests is of utmost importance, although it may be difficult to spot what they are doing as they tend to make it all look so easy! Watching the riding-in is often most valuable, as it is there that corrections will be made to the horse's way of going. It is a good place to see what the rider accepts or considers less acceptable, and how any corrections are made.

It is important to understand that trainers do tackle problems in different ways. Some are strict disciplinarians, while others are more lenient. Strictness is fine so long as the horse improves as a result and is not upset by the correction made.

It is clearly important that a trainer is furthering his horse's future, not destroying it.

Riding dressage is not an easy task. Often work goes wrong, but it is the way problems are tackled that will either take you forward or inhibit progress.

Studying Tests

Studying the tests to be ridden is essential. It is not enough merely to learn them; there is far more to it than that. Every test should be analysed in terms of its demands and its emphasis. For instance, a Preliminary Level test will have the accent placed on balance, straightness, freedom and correctness of the gaits, outline, bend, smooth transitions and good acceptance of the aids.

At Novice Level all the Preliminary work applies, with even more emphasis on regularity, engagement, impulsion, suppleness and accuracy.

By Elementary, a degree of collection is required. Also gait variations, an outline that reflects the further increase of engagement and energy, and a higher level of accuracy.

At Medium Level the horse should show that he is ready to make the transition to Advanced; that all his basic work is well established and that his suppleness permits him to conform to all the demands of the test with fluidity of performance.

Once in Advanced there will be many additional points to consider, as these tests incorporate all movements, and a high degree of accuracy and obedience will be expected.

It is necessary to be fully aware of the requirements of all movements, and never to lose sight of basic principles. The degrees of collection and extension required at each level will need study, also how this is to be achieved from the correct build-up of work.

When studying tests the rider should be aware of the elements which comprise each mark of ten. For example, a lengthened trot on the diagonal will include the quality of the gait, balance, straightness, outline and regularity, and the transitions into and from the lengthening. Therefore, although the actual lengthening will count for the majority of marks, the judge will be taking all these points into consideration.

Another example is when the test demands a medium canter on a diagonal, with flying change at X.
Again, the quality of the canter is paramount – although a high proportion of the mark will be given for the flying change, which should be straight, true and expressive. So, although a judge must constantly compute many points in his mind, he will put emphasis on the most difficult part of the movement.

With experience, the rider will learn to assess his own performance and will be self-critical enough that, when he receives his judging sheet, he will already have a good idea of the probable comments.

Judging and Teaching

Judging is an excellent way to learn, as it provides a different perspective and offers the rider a chance to see the detail of work that the judge sees, and of which he might otherwise be unaware. Naturally, such an appointment should not be accepted without sufficient knowledge and this means having ridden, and preferably trained, a horse to the level being judged. Only then can a judge fully appreciate the rider's point of view and be able to evaluate the work properly.

Being a teacher is an advantage to learning in that, in order to be able to give comprehensible explanations, it is necessary to think in depth. Much can be learned by having to study in detail another person's riding and training capacities, even if that person is a complete novice. An ability to 'ride from the ground' is a useful addition to being able to do so in the saddle.

Teaching also provides the opportunity to watch a huge

variety of horses and riders, from whom much valuable knowledge and experience can be drawn. All such discoveries can be incorporated in some way into the immense store of knowledge needed to be successful in dressage.

Formal teaching does require qualifications and the relevant insurance, but it can be a useful addition to riding for those so inclined.

The Learning Environment

For anyone starting on a dressage career the right environment is essential, not only to their concentration, but also to achieve the right result.

The first essential is to have an appropriate area to school on, whether this be simply a marked-out arena in a field, an all-weather surface or an indoor facility. In an ideal world, the combination of indoor and outdoor facilities is plainly the best, as horse and rider gain the advantage of being able to train all year round. However, many riders do not have such an opportunity, and must make the most of what they have. Nevertheless, unless school movements can be ridden accurately in a routine and consistent manner, the necessary physical and mental development will be retarded.

One of the most important factors is that the surface where the horse is expected to work should be safe, and never hard or slippery. This is vital to the regularity of the gaits and to general development, and it is also necessary to the rider's ability to think positively. A rider who is anxious or too passive will not make his horse work properly.

To start with, peace and quiet is important. Neither horse nor rider will be receptive if there are constant distractions. At a later date during training, certain distractions may be introduced deliberately in order to train the horse to listen to and obey his rider under such conditions. The rider will also need this training so that he learns to distance himself from outside activities.

A dressage rider needs a high degree of rapport with his horse, and this is not acquired only by riding. A suitable stable, and an exercise area which promotes this by providing close association, are also important.

6
Training and Preparation

Although there is bound to be certain variance between methods of different countries, the end result should be the same. Choosing the route is dependent on each person's interpretation, and every individual will add details to his training method as he goes along and learns more. The difficulty lies in not being side-tracked by new ideas; rather, one should evaluate them carefully before adding or discarding them. What is right for one person or horse is not necessarily right for another, so differences are bound to arise. As the saying goes: 'There are many roads to Rome. It does not matter which one you take so long as you get there!'

The Horse's Memory

From a practical point of view the first important consideration is to be aware of the way in which the horse learns his work, and therefore how he should be taught. His overriding attribute is his memory, which is far more acute than ours! He forgets very little – which is an advantage or a disadvantage depending on his experience. If something pleasant happens to him, for which he receives praise, he will clearly be happy about this and will not mind it being repeated. This is why the means we have at our disposal (the aids) must be considered so carefully before they are used! Rough or thoughtless aids, even if not intentional, will register in the horse's mind and become a permanent fixture just as quickly as those given correctly. The association of aids from past experiences can make him either cooperative or opposed to his rider, so it is clear that he should, so far as possible, be given the right instruction in the first place.

On the question of aids for specific movements, the rider must be clear in his mind, not only as to what they are, but also to make sure they are given with complete consistency. If aids are used in this way any repetition of an exercise can be confirmed in the horse's mind, stored in his memory, and instantly recalled in the same situation. Once they have been thoroughly learned, the horse never forgets his rider's aids. The only differences in response that might occur could result from muscles having become stiff or tense, whether from age or lack of regular work.

Even a different rider using the same aids could expect the horse to answer, and a well-trained horse would do so.

In addition to using the right aids, the rider is responsible for making his wishes clear in the way he explains to the horse what he requires. As with any new subject, a simple introduction is necessary; this is then followed by working through various stages of difficulty in a progressive manner.

If a rider uses his intelligence, he should be able to put himself mentally in the horse's place to establish a logical build-up to any exercise. If, for example, the rider wishes to teach the horse a walk pirouette, he must realise that a good pirouette cannot be achieved without collection. Collection requires acceptance of the use of half-halts. Half-halts can only be achieved if the horse is accepting a combined use of legs and hands and is submissive to them. Good collection with elastic, regular steps cannot be arrived at without a good basic walk. This requires straightness, balance and forward momentum, and so on!

From a clear stage-by-stage explanation, the right sort of mental and physical development can be expected, especially if the rider is careful to praise his horse along the way.

School Movements

As previously mentioned, all the school movements are designed to create the right kind of development so that the horse may ultimately be able to perform the Grand Prix test. They should be taught in a way similar to the growth of a tree. Everything grows from the main trunk, and relies on this being strong and well sustained. In other words, the horse's three gaits being correct, straight, balanced, regular and energetic can be thought of as the trunk, with all movements being an extension of this base.

Movements which are ridden accurately contribute greatly to development. This accuracy should vary only in the capacity of the horse to respond at the level of training he has at the time. For instance a novice horse may be shown some leniency, whereas an advanced one is expected to be precise. Not only does the horse develop from correctly ridden exercises; the rider also benefits. His physical strength is built up so that he can sustain effort for long periods, and his concentration levels improve.

School diagrams can be a daunting sight; it is, however, necessary to get to grips with them. Actually riding them is a good way of making them more clear, so long as a check is made from the original drawings. All movements can be ridden properly only if the rider is secure in his position and sits evenly and straight in the saddle, so a constant check should be made when schooling.

When in doubt as to how to proceed with training it can be helpful to consult the test sheets. This provides an insight into what will be required at the various levels.

Some movements cause more trouble than others, with the rider suffering a mental block. In particular, lateral work and flying changes seem to fall into this category. So often they will seem easier to ride on one rein than on the other, or the 'timing' seems impossible to realise. At such moments it may be comforting to remember that this is not unusual. Most people co-ordinate better to one direction, and find the other less easy.

Patience and perseverance are the answer, plus careful attention to the right preparation for that movement. If the horse is in the right position for what he is being asked to do he will be able to answer – which will help his rider also.

Obedience

It should be understood that no horse will learn his work unless he is praised or corrected according to his responses.

Praise, can, of course, be given only if the rider recognises an improvement. This recognition is hard for a novice rider, which is why he needs fairly constant guidance. It is so important that the horse is given a pat on the neck, or praised by his rider's voice, so that confirmation of the right response can be made.

Corrections of incorrect responses are equally important, and the way that these are done can make or break the whole training. It is essential that a correction is made at the time of the mistake so that the horse is not in doubt. All such corrections should be made without roughness or lack of calculation.

Accepting the need for obedience depends largely on the temperament and character of the horse concerned. Therefore each rider must get to know his own animal in order to know how best to deal with him.

Teaching the horse to be obedient can be troublesome, especially if a rider has very high expectations of himself, and finds it unsatisfactory to accept less than the best. Self-criticism is valuable if kept in perspective, but not if it results in impatience and consequent friction. Sometimes, deep-rooted feelings of inadequacy cause a rider to act harshly or without enough thought. This, clearly, is likely to cause the wrong kind of reaction from the horse.

In all cases where a rider expects too high a degree of obedience for the stage of training there may be ensuing problems. Any sort of pressure put on the horse before he is mentally or physically able raises the possibility of subjection rather than co-operation. In dressage one of the objects is to see an obedient horse but, at the same time, he should display his own natural pride and vigour.

Fitness

The importance of fitness for both horse and rider is often underestimated, but lack of it can cause much distress and result in unnecessarily poor performances.

Although skilled practitioners make dressage riding look easy, it is exceedingly hard work and it is necessary to have a programme for fitness as well as for training. In truth, most fitness comes from riding every day and being consistent.

Drifting around the school without enough thought or physical energy can only produce a lethargic outcome. After an initial 'warming up', horse and rider must *work*! The rider should constantly check his position while also considering how his horse is going every step of the way! His brain should be active; thinking ahead, planning his next move, carefully initiating that plan and then analysing the result. The horse should be energetic and alert, listening to the aids and responding to them. From this kind of activity of mind and body physical condition is built. Only by the right muscle development will horse and rider be able to form a real partnership, able to sustain effort for the duration of a test.

Some riders do incorporate roadwork or lungeing into their fitness regime. Whatever the individual's preference, it must be backed by the right kind of feeding and care for the horse in the stable, and by proper diet and exercise for the rider.

Preparing for the Show

TACK AND TURNOUT

There is no doubt that it can really boost a rider's confidence if he and his horse are 'looking the part'. The right tack for the job, clothes and general presentation are very important.

There is so much choice nowadays that it would be unwise of me to give any specific suggestions as to the type of saddlery or rider's clothing. However, as a judge, I admit to a preference for conservative attire for the rider! There are some items of clothing that do seem less than appropriate – and some are almost an insult to the horse!

Saddles must, of course, fit the size of the horse and the physical build of the rider. Bridles should suit the type of horse and the size of head; heavy leather is unsuitable on a small-boned head, as is thin leather on a large head.

Although marks are not given for turnout it is very important to create the right impression. Horses who are unplaited, with unpulled tails, or riders with untidy hair are clearly not giving themselves the best chances.

THOUGHTS ON TRAVELLING

Transporting horses, whether in a lorry or trailer, is an acquired skill and one that is essential to the horse's well-being and the rider's nerves! Having a 'bad traveller' is altogether unnerving and, in any case, may cause damage to either the animal or the vehicle.

Generally, I would say that horses do not start out as poor travellers, but they may become upset as a result of thoughtless or ignorant driving. The kind of thing that upsets them is sudden acceleration or braking, and being swung round corners. This kind of carelessness on the part of the driver is so often reflected in that person's riding also! Those who think what they want to do, and at what speed they need to drive in order for the horse to retain his balance, have the same attitude when riding.

There is no point in stubbornly expecting a horse who is nervous simply to improve. Once he has been frightened, he will never forget the experience. Only by adjusting his travelling space and by driving with more care will he overcome his fears.

Many horses are troublesome to load; some are nervous and others simply 'bolshie'. It is important to make the right assessment so that the correct approach is made. Nervous horses do need encouragement, reassurance and patience. The more stubborn ones must be made to understand that they have no alternative!

Making this assessment is not always simple, but knowing the horse's temperament and character will usually provide the answer. Being patient is often exceedingly difficult, especially if it is pouring with rain or time is slipping away. For this reason it is wise to practise loading, so that the time factor can be gauged.

Sometimes, perversely, the difficult horse decides not to be difficult after all! One is then left with an abundance of time that is not really required. This, however, is far better than running late, and allows for a steady journey and calm nerves.

Allowing enough time for a journey is, in any case, hard to assess as so many other factors, such as roadworks, etc., can be involved. However, it is always better to arrive at a show early and give the horse time to settle. A good test will not be accomplished if the rider is on edge or the horse insufficiently ridden-in.

Another potential trauma lies in deciding what clothing the horse should travel in. If he is too hot he may sweat up or become agitated. If too cold, his coat will be staring and he may catch a chill. Since balancing in a lorry or trailer is hard work for the horse, he may 'run up' as a result. His clothing can either add to his problems or help him, and only a sensitive approach by his owner, and trial and error, will provide the right answers.

EQUIPMENT CHECKLISTS

In all preparation for a competition it is important to pave the way for calmness on the morning of the show. Keeping checklists is one way of reducing the stress of trying to remember what to take. I have prepared some lists for inclusion in this chapter but as I am not infallible there may well be other items to add to them!

The Horse

Warm day-rug.
Sheet.
Blanket.
Anti-sweat rug.
Roller and/or surcingle. Pad to go under same.
Waterproof exercise sheet.
Exercise blanket.
(All the above dependent on the weather, of course.)
Travelling bandages.
Exercise bandages or boots.
Padding to go under exercise bandages.
Knee pads.
Hock boots.
Tail guard.
Headcollar and rope.
Spare rope.
Knife to cut rope in emergency.
Hoof oil and brush or similar.
Hoof pick.
Grooming kit, including sponge and scissors.
Plaiting kit.
Veterinary essentials; wound powder, cotton wool, thermometer, etc.
2 Buckets or 1 bucket and manger.
Water.
Fly spray.
Spare set of shores (if travelling abroad).
Enough feed, hay, etc., for the trip.
Haynets (tied to string).
Shovel and skip.
Saddle(s) depending on number of horses.
Girth and spare.
Stirrups and spare leathers.
Leather punch.
Saddlecloth or numnah.
Snaffle bridle and/or double bridle as required.
Spare reins.

Other essentials
Money.
Sunglasses.
Tablets for headache!
The tests to be ridden.
Rule book.
Show schedule.
Directions to the show.
Lunch and flasks.
Garden chairs or shooting stick.
A towel, in case you get soaked!
(If the dog is going too don't forget his water, food and lead.)

Rider's clothing
Cap or top hat.
Hairnet (if female).
Safety pins.
Stock or tie.
Tie pin.
Appropriate shirts.
Clothes brush.
Jacket or jackets and/or tail coat.
Gloves (plus 1 spare pair).
Breeches (2 pairs if competition lasts more than one day).
Boots (spare pair very useful if weather is wet).
Boot pulls.
Boot jack.
Spurs.
Schooling whip.
Clothes to change into after competition.
Mackintosh.
Wellingtons.
Umbrella.

So far as clothing for the test is concerned, it must comply with the rules for that class and should be clean – at least at the start of the day! It should also fit as well as possible.

Clothing that is too tight can be very inhibiting, while something that is too loose or baggy does not convey the right impression.

Hats worn on the back of the head give the rider a very amateurish look, and untidy hair of any kind is strictly taboo!

Spurs must be worn correctly, that is with the arm of the spur level with the seam on the heel of the boot. Straps can be adjusted to make this possible. Spurs worn too low are ineffective and incorrect.

After each show it is a good idea to leave those items that can be left in the lorry (tidily), so that they are ready for next time. If clothing has to be sent to the cleaners do get this done in plenty of time to avoid panic at the last minute. Thinking ahead is well worthwhile, and really does save unnecessary agonies on the day.

7
Going to the Show

I know that there are few people who are not in some way affected by nerves prior to, and on the morning of, the show. How the rider feels in the morning can depend very much on the night he has just had! I can remember, only too well, the sleepless nights beforehand spent mentally riding and re-riding the test. I also recall vividly the nightmare of arriving at the show minus the bridle, the boots or the breeches!

There is also the pathological worry of the possibility of finding the horse lame in the morning, or the lorry refusing to start! All such demands upon the nervous energies have a thoroughly destructive effect on sleep, leaving the brain sluggish and the body lethargic.

Although such nights may not be entirely eliminated, there are some ways in which their influence can be minimised. The first is to ensure that the tests ridden are well ingrained in the memory, having been thoroughly learned well in advance. The second is by knowing that all check-lists have been checked and double-checked. The third is by having the knowledge that all training has been thorough, and all necessary preparations made. Lastly, have confidence in your alarm clock!

The Morning Routine

If the morning routine has been thought out well beforehand, the actual execution of it can be done almost on 'automatic pilot'. This gives the body time to adjust to an early rising, and allows a gradual build-up of energies.

All practical aspects such as feeding, grooming, mucking out, plaiting and so on should have been organised in a way that suits each person mentally, and allows the horse the best chance to start the day in a relaxed manner.

Even if the thought of eating breakfast is not top priority at this time of day, time should be allowed for something, otherwise a hideous void in the stomach later in the day will spoil concentration, and you will be short of energy.

The horse, of course, should have been fed early enough so that he can eat his breakfast calmly. If he senses the outing and will not finish up do not worry; he can be 'topped up' later. Some people like to plait up the night before a show, which does save a rush in the morning, but the horse will know something is up and may have a fretful night.

With older campaigners, a show routine may be different than that for the newcomer – and this applies to both parties! Anyone new to the game will have their apprehensions on a show morning and these are soon transmitted to the horse, but the better the preparation, the more possible it is to be calm.

Because all horses are different it is important to be sensitive to their needs. Some will not bat an eyelid at being taken from their stable at 4 a.m. and loaded into the lorry. Others may need a few minutes on the lunge to remove energies that may cause restlessness on the journey. Such things should be allowed for.

The moment of loading up is crucial to the whole morning. If it goes without a hitch, the day can begin with everyone in the right mood. To achieve this it is a good idea to make sure that the lorry or trailer is parked somewhere suitable with a good run up; no slippery approach and not directly away from equine friends. Also, provide some lighting inside in order that the horse can see where he is going, and do not ask him to go into too small a space. Once he is inside do not thoughtlessly slam up the ramp, or set off like a maniac, but start off sensibly so that he can get his 'sea legs'.

The Journey and Arrival at the Show

Allowing enough time is the key to a relatively stress-free journey. Being late is hopeless, and simply causes irritability and anxiety. Without being a pessimist it is wise to remember that vehicles will break down or have punctures, and the council will have dug up your road, causing delays! Even if arrival at the show is far too early, this is better than missing the class. Knowing the route or having a good map reader is essential. It is always best to avoid narrow lanes or heavy traffic if at all possible.

Some horses are very good travellers, which makes the journey quite relaxed, but there are others who cannot tolerate travelling and, in such cases, each person must get to know the best way of making their horse less anxious. This sometimes means giving extra space or altering the travelling position. Most horse need to splay their legs slightly in order to balance, so narrow compartments can cause trouble. It is important to get the travelling details right so that riders and horse can arrive at the show in a calm state.

On a long journey, the horse or horses should be checked to see that nothing is wrong. Rugs do slip sometimes, or bandages become loose.

Depending on the time needed for riding-in, the arrival should be at least one hour before the riding-in period, so that rider and horse can rest after the journey. Try to park the lorry near to the arena, if permitted, to cut down on exhausting walking to and fro. Check that the horse has not sweated up and that he is comfortable.

Arriving in plenty of time allows for a restoring cup of coffee before going to look at the arena where the test is to be ridden. This is very important. All arenas have their quirks, such as being uneven, having wet or muddy areas, having posters or banners that could be distracting, unusual markers, or tubs of flowers.

The surface is obviously of major interest but there may be many other points to consider. Indoor arenas can be particularly distracting for the horse and it is wise to be prepared, so that if the horse does not go as well as he does at home the rider can put it down to necessary experience.

In order to avoid turning up late for the class, always check the timetable. Also, find out the number of the rider before you and keep an eye on the general proceedings. Finally, make sure that all items of clothing and tack are to hand so that there is no last-minute panic.

Riding-in

So far as riding-in is concerned, there can be no set formula. Each horse is so different from another that one cannot be laid down. Much depends on the fitness and temperament of the horse in question. Some can be ready in a very short time, while others can literally take hours. The exact time required for each horse will only be discovered by practice. Mistakes and disappointment on the way are only to be expected; experience will provide an answer. However, there are certain points to consider with any horse.

In the first instance, any horse will need time to adjust to the atmosphere of the show, and cannot be expected to settle and work until he has had a good look round. Some people like to put the horse on the lunge first for this reason. He will then need a warming-up period to supple his muscles so that real work can follow. During this time the rider is also becoming 'tuned in', both mentally and physically, to the job ahead.

Sometimes it is very difficult to get the necessary concentration going. If the riding-in area is in a wide open space, the horse will be less inclined to settle as he may want to look around. If he is used to working in a school this is very distracting for him and irritating for his rider. Alternatively, the riding-in area may be in a school where everything feels very cramped because of the other horses working. It is always hard to capture the feel you really want with so much activity all around, but this is one of the hazards of competition and can only be overcome by being 'out there doing it'!

When the horse has become attentive, he can be taken through his normal routine. Some accent may be put on certain areas of training. It may be necessary to repeat an exercise several times if it is not quite right, or to practise some movement that has given trouble in the past.

Reaching the right level of concentration is hard work but has a huge bearing on results. It is necessary to avoid looking around at the other competitors, and to give full attention to your own animal. Sometimes it is necessary to be a little ruthless in order to maintain the circle of concentration built around you. Unfortunately, the average person is often unaware of a rider's need to be oblivious to his surroundings and may cause interruption by some well-meant greeting or remark. Part of mental training involves the ability to acknowledge such moments with a smile, or nod, without allowing the concentration level to fall.

During riding-in there may be moments when the partnership seems to be falling apart through the stress of the occasion. If possible, find a quiet corner, have a rest period and think about what is causing the problem. It is important not to lose confidence at this time nor to upset the trust the horse has in you.

A great aid to keeping calm is to have a friend or partner watching out for any changes in the timetable. For instance, a quick judge may bring the times forward, and a slow one can make the class late. It is very important to have progress reports in order to adjust the riding-in period. If the class runs early for some reason, provided the horse is sufficiently prepared, do not keep the judge waiting!

Running late is a different matter and, sadly, this can completely upset a young horse or a rider new to the job. It is very hard to bring the horse to his peak at the right moment, and to be strong mentally and physically. At such a time the art of relaxation is very important. Loosen tense muscles, breathe properly, re-focus the mind and quietly begin again!

Show Psychology

It is quite usual for any competitor to glance around a showground and panic, thinking that all the other competitors are more competent and have better-trained horses! Experience, however, will prove that 'all that glitters is not gold!' Those riders who appear to be so competent are probably as terrified as everyone else, and those beautiful looking horses are just as likely to misbehave as any other. Even the greatest expert can have troubles in the arena!

There are also other thoughts to contend with, such as catching sight of someone sitting beside the arena with whom there has been a personal disagreement.This can be very off-putting. And, of course, there is the psychological disadvantage of riding against the 'names'.

So far as the 'names' are concerned, it may seem that they always win, or the judges mark them up.What should be remembered is that, in general, these experts have become 'names' because they are the best, and their position at the head of a class will be a result of much hard work and experience. It is no good at all being downhearted when riding against the experts. In fact, the aim should be to get as close to their marks as possible, and one day to overtake them and become a 'name' too!

A real desire to do well and to suppress all psychological interference will pump up the adrenalin so that self-consciousness, or lack of confidence, is pushed into the background.

Seeing a judge sitting at C who, last time he judged you, gave a low mark, can be unnerving. Tackle this by believing that, while he may remember how the horse went last time, he is really hoping to give better marks this time – for this is exactly what he will be thinking. No judge *wants* to give low marks.

Every competitor knows about the dreaded 'pain barrier' caused by old or current injuries, or by lack of fitness.Pain certainly can be a block to success but, with mental resolve, it is amazing how physical agony can be pushed into the background.(In spite of this it is perhaps unwise in most circumstances to compete knowing that an injury or physical problem will prevent the best effort. Being up to the mark is important.)

The effect of unpleasant experiences in the past can clearly play on the mind, and this can cause psychological problems. This remark applies to the horse, too! Certain venues can be responsible for this reaction, as some seem to present problems that others do not. Every rider dreads his horse sensing a 'bogy' either in, or next to, an arena. If this happens, on returning to that arena, the imaginary fear may be remembered.

Breaking patterns of behaviour in either ourselves or our horses is not easy. Not only does it require skill, but also a great deal of trust. It is natural for any rider to fear that he will let himself or his horse down by doing something foolish. Once you have made a silly mistake this should prevent a recurrence, but in a contrary way it can actually cause it to happen again, merely because it is present in the mind. Blocking out errors is never simple, but try to be strong-minded and look ahead.

One way to boost confidence is simply to believe that you are the best! This does not, of course, mean 'showing off', because this may put too much pressure on the horse and will probably result in a shallow quality of riding. Also, too much practice at certain movements merely to impress onlookers outside the ring often makes the horse too sour to do them again inside it!

Complacency is also a mistake! So often, outside the arena, all seem to be going well, causing the rider to be lulled into a false sense of security. When the test starts, both horse and rider may find each other not in tune after all. It is therefore so important when riding-in to assess thoroughly how the horse is going and to adjust to each situation as it arises.

Riding several tests in one day needs an experienced and confident approach. There is inevitably a sense of anticlimax after the first, and much effort has to be raised in order to 'psyche' yourself up again.

In The Arena

Waiting for the judge to give the signal to start the test is always agonizing. At this point, try to keep the mind focused on how the horse should feel. Do not put him under extra pressure. Keep calm and remember to breathe!

Having ridden in at A, keep your eye on the C marker, not on the judge. Think about the initial halt, if the test demands one, and have the right or left turn at C firmly in your mind.

The surface may not feel as expected, but concentrate on the horse and think about the movement being ridden.Do not be in a hurry. Work the horse as if you were at home, making corrections if necessary. If you have to give a strong half-halt to improve balance or control, the judge will understand. If the gait needs activating, give a quick flick of the whip.This will improve response and give you more confidence that the horse is going forwards. It will also make the movements easier.

Think about the aids. Any that are too obvious will create a poor impression and make you feel inadequate, as the horse will no doubt resist them. Make sure that the horse responds to leg aids with the help of the whip if necessary, and use the rein aids intelligently so that the horse constantly 'listens'.

Make sure that every movement is started and ended clearly (though not abruptly) and be sure that your own mental preparation is adequately transmitted to the horse. This is essential in order that the performance is not stilted, but flows smoothly. Rushing through a test may be a temptation but prevents the horse from being able to do his work in a balanced way.

In the back of your mind, you will be aware of how the test is going, but you must keep thinking ahead. If the test is going well it is easy to become nervous so that, at any moment, it may all go wrong. If it is not going too well it is just as easy to give up hope. Neither attitude must be allowed to develop. Concentration on what is happening at the time and on what is coming next will help to overcome such nerves. Mistakes will happen and confidence can be shaken. Always put what has gone on already to the back of the mind and focus all your attention on what is coming. Even with mistakes tests can still be won; it is not the end of everything.

During tests there will be many distractions. The weather is certainly responsible for some of them. If it is wet and windy and the arena has blown away it is still possible to continue! If your hat blows off or you drop your whip, just carry on! If sweat is pouring off you and you are going scarlet in the face this does not matter if you still manage to ride effectively. The horse may suddenly do something unexpected or uncharacteristic. Be ready to recover and pick up the pieces!

At the end of the test try to look agreeable, even if it has been a disaster. You will not be the only one this has happened to; the judge himself has very probably experienced the same thing and, even if he cannot give good marks, he will at least be sympathetic.

One can feel very lonely in the arena and mistakes can seem like major catastrophes. Just try to remember that your horse is your partner and that although you may fail sometimes, if there is a strong bond and a desire to go on, the loss of one competition is a triviality!

Fatigue and the Next Test

Dressage riding is extremely hard work and competition adds an even greater burden. At the end of a test the competitor may feel drained of all energy and thought. Luckily this is only temporary! It is surprising how quickly the body can bounce back after a short rest, especially if there is another test to ride. Rising out of an anaesthesia of exhaustion is hard, but the brain soon reactivates, sending out appropriate messages to the body so that effort becomes possible once more.

Sometimes a second test is easier to ride since some of the unwanted tensions have gone.The test then provides the necessary mental stimulation required to overcome any physical sluggishness.

8
The Test

Judge's Expectations

In all tests, each judge will hope to see the rider and horse perform according to the picture he holds in his mind. If he can award good marks he will be delighted! Not only is his job much easier, but it is good for the competitor also.

He will hope to see the technical points within the test enhanced by skilful, bold riding that gives the work life and expression. At the various levels he will expect to see degrees of balance, energy, collection and extension appropriate to that level, and that the horse shows good suppleness and is submissive to all his rider's requests. Additionally, he will hope that horse and rider will display the unity and harmony that can exist only if training has been correct.

A judge may also expect a degree of respect, as he has trained long and hard himself to achieve his position. Without him there would be no competition, so he is an essential element in the procedure and justifiably should be shown consideration. Although he cannot please everyone in the class, he will be doing his best to evaluate all performances fairly and accurately. Despite this, he can only give his opinion, and he will be aware that those competitors who have lost may well criticise his judgement. Nevertheless, he is prepared to take this responsibility, and to suffer the exhaustion of judging a long class, but at the end of it all he will expect some appreciation.

Rider's Expectations and Reactions

Every competitor should be aware of the judge's hopes; indeed he aspires to them himself! Achieving them, of course, is what training and competing are all about.

The rider can help himself by initially trying to present the judge with the right picture. His body language can give a pretty accurate indication of how he is feeling. If his facial expression is apologetic, dejected, or cross this is a 'give away' and his attitude may well be reflected in his riding! On the other hand, calm determination will give the rider a confident air, helping him to ride with purpose and to send the right signals to the judge.

Personal expectations differ in each individual case, depending on character. This applies not just to dressage, but in life generally. Those who have high ideals will constantly strive for them, being dissatisfied with themselves if they cannot match up to them. Others are less ambitious and settle for lower levels of attainment. There are also those who inwardly desire a lot but lack confidence, and expect too little as a result. A trainer or knowledgeable person may be able to bring more out of such people. Then there are those who just expect to do well but are oblivious of the need to work, or simply lack the talent. When such people do not win they blame everyone else but themselves!

Every dressage competitor's aim will be to achieve a high percentage of marks. To accomplish this is not easy and sometimes expectations are too high. It may make a rider feel better if he puts the blame for low or average percentages on the judges, some of whom seem consistently to give low marks. It is true that some judges are more generous with marks than others, just as some people are more generous-minded, while others are less tolerant. However, while it may be hard going under a tough judge and gaining a low percentage, this makes little difference to the outcome of a class, since the winner will be the winner in any case. Therefore, rather than feeling bitter about such judging, it may be better to take the view that the judge in question simply has a rather high standard, and it does no-one any harm to have a shake-up from time to time.

Competition necessarily means experiencing a mixture of success and defeat. Success early on is often described as 'beginner's luck'. This can happen, but it can merely be that, because at this stage expectation is not high, the rider is more relaxed, allowing mind and body to work well together. Once there is 'something to lose', expectations of oneself and others leads to tensions, which are immediately felt by the horse.

Staying 'at the top' is hard and it will not last; there is bound to be a slide sooner or later! Any rider reaching the zenith of his career must expect his reign to end sometime. This does not, of course, mean accepting the fact as a permanent state: any true competitor will want to fight back. Defeat of any kind is hard to accept, in fact it is intolerable! Outwardly, however, it should be accepted gracefully. Inwardly, there may be a burning fury: not at the judge or the horse but merely against the fact of defeat.

Of course, all expectations of success must relate to the level of training. It would clearly be foolish to expect to do well at Medium Level if the horse has only been trained for a short while at this level at home. In fact it would be true to say that the horse should only be expected to do well in a test of the level *below* the one he his working on at home.

Disappointment at a poor performance can cause a bad reaction, either by being disagreeable, or by punishing the horse. Obviously neither will be beneficial and such response can even get a rider a bad name, so it should be avoided at all costs. Whenever there is anger or frustration it is a good idea to go somewhere quiet, where things can be thought through and calm regained.

RELAXATION

Being keyed up and mentally primed is essential to every competitor, but this must be achieved without causing physical tensions, which inhibit performance. On the other hand, the art of being able to relax is very difficult to master.

It either seems unachievable or, if successful, causes a total 'switch off'!

Mastering the art requires practice and experience. Being able to concentrate is part of the answer, since the mind is then directed towards the horse and the feel he is giving. If concentration can be maintained the body will react, following the horse's movement with sufficient muscle power but without rigidity.

When actually riding the test there is much to concentrate on, so it is not easy to remember to breathe properly or to think about keeping joints flexible. If these points are forgotten, muscles can gradually become tense, breathing shallow and arms and hands restrictive. Any stiffness will, in turn, affect the use of the aids, so that transmissions become distorted. If the messages the horse receives are not the normal ones, they will confuse him, and he will not be able to respond as he should. With experience, however, the rider will become more confident and this will produce a calm and relaxed attitude, allowing mind and body to gain cohesion.

CONFIDENCE

To be able to ride with flair and inspire confidence in the horse, the rider will need to be sure of his own abilities. This confidence will derive from past success, which will make him more certain that he can win. Also, he may have the backing of a trainer whom he trusts, who can assure him of his capability. The other key factor is the horse himself, who provides the feeling that the whole experience is being shared, and that he is doing his part.

Those people with inborn confidence have a big advantage, as they do not doubt their powers and can remain cool in a show atmosphere. Of course, no-one is invincible and even the most cocksure must take the knocks, but people of this type usually bounce back quickly.

The less sure one is of oneself, the more possible it is for doubt to destroy any positive thoughts one might have. Add to this a churning stomach; a feeling of wanting to be sick; or trembling knees, and the recipe for failure is there.

Of course, it is difficult to convince yourself that all will be well, especially as there are two entities to take into account. It is important, however, to believe you can win, but such a thought can only be present with the knowledge that both the horse and the training are good enough.

Although natural talent is a big asset, other assets must be acquired, especially the all-important determination. There is no doubt that this counts for a lot. Clearly, years of practice help boost a rider's confidence in himself, especially if he makes good headway. He will learn through trial and error which techniques work best and how to pick up marks – not waste them. His mental attitude will strengthen together with his performance.

Being 'on top of your game' is the biggest boost: knowing that the training has reached a level where it is secure and unlikely to fail.

MISTAKES AND ERRORS OF COURSE

In any test there are bound to be mistakes; the occasional 'crossed line' or moments when something is not as it should be. At such a time it is crucial to be in control mentally so that the quickest recovery possible can be made. If concentration is on maximum power, a momentary lapse will not become a collapse!

Making a mistake is distracting; it upsets the flow and the train of thought. It requires quick thinking and firm resolve to ensure that the whole performance does not disintegrate. There are certain movements – tempi changes for example – where an error can become compounded purely by the difficulty of the exercise. In such instances it is important to remember that any rider panic can only make matters worse.

Dwelling on the mistake is out of the question. The horse, as well as the rider, will have been upset by the error and the rider must focus quickly on bringing everything back together. If the partnership has been well formed, a recovery can be achieved quite quickly. Experienced riders are very good at 'covering up' errors, or nipping them in the bud so quickly that very few marks are lost, but this is a skill acquired through much practice.

On the whole, making repeated or substantial mistakes shows a lack of preparation for that particular test, and this should be a warning to the rider that his work needs review.

Actual errors of course are everyone's nightmare. It is all too easy to panic, causing the brain to 'scramble' and momentarily cease to function clearly. At such a moment do not be in too much of a hurry to continue. Listen carefully to the judge's reminder of the route and prepare the horse properly before carrying on.

Whatever happens regarding mistakes or errors in the arena, it is important to remember that the horse's future is at stake and that nothing should be done that might damage progress.

Whilst on the subject of mistakes, I should perhaps make further mention of commanders (see Chapter 4 – Learning Tests) since it is after an error that a rider is likely to say: 'I should have had the test commanded!' Of course, this can be very helpful, especially if one is competing in several tests on the same day. However, the 'commander' should have a clear voice, be able to combat noise and weather, and must call each movement in plenty of time, but not too early. This requires considerable concentration, and you must choose your 'commander' carefully if you are to avoid the frustration and indignity of going wrong despite having the test commanded. Therefore, while it can be useful and reassuring to have a test commanded, no-one should become reliant on it.

AFTER THE TEST

Once the test is over the rider may experience a feeling of quiet satisfaction at a job well done, or he may have a niggling worry that, despite attempts to hide flaws, the judge will have seen them anyway!

A win provides a feeling of euphoria that can last for days and gives a good incentive to continue work. Losing, however, leaves one feeling empty and deflated; sometimes disheartened. At such a time, some serious thought should be given to what went wrong, so that a decision can be made as to whether it was caused by the pressure of the day, the different environment, or an actual flaw in the training that needs attention.

Because everyone wants to be 'top dog', the attitude of other competitors can bring about some problems to contend with. Human nature, being what it is, does sometimes produce unpleasantness in such forms as jealousy, sarcasm and criticism. Knowing another person's opinion of the horse, your riding or the training can be off-putting, and can even lead you in the wrong direction.

While you should not dwell on such attitudes, it is necessary to be aware of the reactions of others and to realise that sometimes comments are made out of envy.

Judges' criticism is, of course, a different matter. The sheets should be read carefully, however low the marks. By studying them the rider will see that the judge has given comments calculated to show the rider what he needs to improve. Even if you dispute the judge's opinion it is worth a little effort to try to understand what he saw, or thought he saw, as there is often more than a grain of truth there.

However satisfied one is with the performance, win or lose, it is important to listen to the opinion of others, provided they offer constructive advice, and to keep an open mind and realise that improvements can always be made.

Putting a bad result behind you is never easy, especially if you feel it is undeserved. What is most important is to look ahead, to face up to the truth, and not to make excuses.

9
Acting on Results

The course of action a rider decides to take following a competition is of great importance, as it can either improve or upset subsequent training. Even if a win has been achieved, this will still need contemplation. Think whether it was a good win, with everything going as planned, or whether it was a lucky win!

Questioning Yourself

Most deliberation comes from unsatisfactory results, because causes must be found. First of all, it is necessary to question yourself about a number of issues. To begin with, the actual riding of the test should be looked at. The rider should try in all honesty to decide whether he was really capable of riding the test as it needed to be ridden. Following on from this, there are many specific points to consider:

Did you sit properly throughout?

Were the aids applied as they should have been?

Was the horse given every chance to do his best?

Was the preparation before each movement properly planned?

Did lack of experience and technique let you down?

Did the horse seem unhappy with the bit or bits being used?

Were either of you not fit enough to sustain effort?

Was the test too demanding?

Did you try to ride too many tests?

Does the horse need more experience at smaller shows to get used to a show atmosphere?

Should you train more 'in company'?

Did you just 'dry up' because of nerves?

Is the horse really suitable for what you want to do?

Does he have the right temperament?

Is the home training area satisfactory?

Are you with the right trainer?

Each individual will no doubt have many other points to consider.

So far as riding is concerned, it is important to be honest about ability. Every competitor wants to progress but, unless the capacity to ride a specific test is there, much disappointment will follow. The trainer is the best person to advise on the level of the test to be attempted.

Tack, especially the right bit or bits, is an important matter, but I am bound to say that poor results are more often blamed on having used the wrong bit, than on the poor quality of its use!

Horses who misbehave at a show generally do so from excitement and merely need more experience of that situation. Practice at home, riding with others, can help this problem.

Becoming rigid with nerves is always a hazard, and one which can plague a competitor all his life! After many years of practice the rider will learn how to control himself and cope with ring nerves.

It is obviously unwise to enter a horse in a class unless he has a good chance of performing all the work well – otherwise he is bound to struggle. His ability to perform the movements involved depends on his training, scope and temperament. If these are in doubt, aims or goals may have to be modified.

Points To Avoid

OVER-CONFIDENCE

Becoming over-confident in the light of success is something to be wary of. For one thing, it can bring about complacency, so that insufficient thought or effort is put into the training. Secondly, instead of promoting an open mind, it may cause a person to believe that their way is the only way – which prevents further learning.

Conning oneself is also a dangerous pastime! It is very easy at times to be convinced that everything is all right whereas, in reality, it is sub-standard.

Judges are sometimes 'conned' by a big-moving horse who is built in a 'round' shape. His training can seem better than it is, merely because he has balanced, rhythmic gaits. He may gain high marks early in his career but, unfortunately, this can give his rider a false picture, making him believe that it will inevitably carry on in the higher levels. Of course, it may, but so often this erroneous belief results in lovely horses failing to progress up the scale. The truth is, however much natural talent a horse displays at the start of his career, unless he is also trained well, he will fail later on.

PANIC

Poor results in competition can also cause the sort of panic that makes a rider try to alter his riding, or his horse's training, in such a way as he thinks will suit a particular judge. Even worse, he may try to vary his work to suit several different judges! Put down on paper this sounds ridiculous, but many have tried the idea nonetheless.

It could be argued that, if there were no variation within

the judging system, this sort of outlook would be avoided. What must be accepted, however, is an inevitable degree of difference in individual concepts of perfection. No-one can state categorically that, given two horses of the same standard, one is better than the other, unless mistakes are made. Thus each judge will make his own evaluation, and his emphasis may differ from that of his co-judge.

At any rate the rider can see from this that changing his training as described is asking for trouble. He must believe in himself and what he is doing while, at the same time, being always willing to learn.

It is important to take the blame for failure so long as this does not develop into such self-criticism that the rider feels totally inadequate and demoralised. A rider must possess faith in himself, and certainly in his horse, if goals are to be attained.

INAPPROPRIATE RESPONSE TO CRITICISM

In competition there can be many sources of criticism, some helpful, some destructive. Each rider must evaluate remarks made to him and accept or discard them. It is a help to be thick-skinned so that one is not upset by some of the less sensitive comments made! Some people invite criticism, but have a clever way of brushing it aside. One question I have often heard from competitors leaving the arena is: 'How do you think my horse went? I thought he went really well!' It is difficult to give any helpful advice in response to such a contradictory question!

Judges' comments necessarily sound critical because they are made to justify low marks, but they are intended to direct the rider's attention to the cause of a problem. Underlining at the end of the test may seem rather curt, but time often does not permit anything else. Sometimes criticisms may seem unjustified or unnecessarily harsh, but a judge can only mark what he sees at the time, which may not coincide with the rider's knowledge of his horse's improvement. Of course, some judges are less knowledgeable than others. However, all criticism, even from your worst enemy, should be assessed to see if it has any merit.

The End Marks

Because there is an enthusiasm to see what marks a judge has given for the various movements, there can sometimes be a lack of appreciation of the importance of the collective marks, which are indeed a summary of the whole test. In consideration of this fact, I felt it might be helpful to analyse these in more detail.

THE PACES, RHYTHM AND REGULARITY

To gain a good mark in this section is absolutely essential, as it tells the rider whether the horse's paces are good enough for the job, and whether they are being developed in the right way.

Any mention by the judge of loss of correct sequence is a very serious matter. If this happens it will be necessary to 'go back to the drawing board' and put right whatever is wrong. If this is not done the rider will be attempting to build his work on clay instead of rock!

Losses of rhythm are also serious, but can normally be corrected quite easily by adjusting balance or speed.

Irregularity is more crucial, because this indicates a developing stiffness, tension or resistance.

IMPULSION

There are many misconceptions regarding the terms 'desire to move forwards' and 'to go forwards freely'! Some interpret this as allowing the horse a free rein, but this merely encourages him to go on his forehand and speed up as he chooses. Others think of it as driving the horse on at all costs, without sufficient regard for balance and rhythm.

In fact the horse cannot go properly forwards, nor will he desire to do so, until he has learned to be 'connected'. That is to say he must use his hindquarters energetically, be supple through his back and submissive in his mouth. Once he has accepted the feeling of being brought together by his rider's leg and hand aids, he will have the inclination to make the desired response. He should then be rewarded by being controlled sympathetically to allow whatever degree of momentum is required at the time.

If the 'connection' is satisfactory the horse will work in a 'round', supple outline, which enables him to move elastically and be flexible in all joints. Effective energy derives from the ability of the rider to engage the horse's hindquarters so that they work under his body, giving them the power to lift the body mass and take him forwards.

SUBMISSION

At all times, when ridden, the horse should attend to his rider and obey his wishes, but he should not be expected to do this – nor can he – unless the rider himself is disciplined and mentally alert.

If the horse thoroughly understands his work and has been properly prepared for it; is bitted correctly and ridden sympathetically, he should be prepared to submit to his rider's requests. Submission that is obtained from the use of sharp spurs or strong bits usually generates resistances. The horse who has been trained with patience and rapport will be willing and calm, happy to accept his bridle and all other aids.

POSITION OF THE RIDER AND EFFECT OF THE AIDS

It is of course important that the rider should sit correctly, otherwise his influence over the horse is likely to be unsatisfactory. What is even more important, however, is that the rider should be able to influence his horse in such a way that he puts him in a position whereby it is easier for the horse to do what is being asked of him, rather than to resist. No rider should expect to get a good mark for his riding unless he has given his horse the best chance, and has proved his training by getting the right result.

Planning for the Future

Provided that a person is mentally strong he will not be put off by setbacks, but will instead formulate his plans for improvement.

There may be many reasons for re-thinking the training. Some solutions are quite simple, for example adjusting the horse's feeding and exercising programme to improve fitness, or cutting down on the amount of short feed if he is consistently too exuberant. Training problems need more thought in depth to determine whether faults lie in the basics, or whether there were merely superficial problems on the day.

Correcting fundamentals will take time, and there is no point in rushing back into the arena too soon. It the rider's own research does not come up with satisfactory answers, professional help should be sought.

DEVELOPING TECHNIQUE

The essence of riding a test is about putting the horse into a position where he can best do what is asked of him. This involves the greatest attention to detail, plus the ability to control every step. It is not therefore something that can be picked up in five minutes, but is learned by practising movements over and over again for a long period.

The degree of control needed, not only over the horse but also over one's own riding, is hard to explain. It is not a question of merely sitting correctly and maintaining contact with legs and hands, although this is a start; it is more a question of becoming bonded physically, so that all movements between rider and horse are as one. This unity permits an awareness of any need to increase or decrease tensions of contact so that the horse is controlled, but is free to carry himself.

The actual detail of riding movements with the necessary precision is dependent on elasticity, and the submissiveness of the horse to his rider's aids. This is gained by a good understanding of the movements and how the horse should be 'set up' for them. Any weak links in the chain such as crookedness, one-sidedness, or the poor position of the rider can prevent the development of the right technique.

Anything that might cause the horse to make his own decisions rather than listen to his rider's directions is clearly no good, but sometimes it is hard to come to this realisation because of long-term fault, to which a rider has become accustomed. The sort of thing to which I refer is a habit, such as sitting to one side, collapsing the back or waist, looking down, or tipping the head to the side, which has been present for some time. This, inevitably, will cause difficulties of control.

Much can be learned about technique by watching the experts but in the final analysis it will be the horse who will teach you the most!

SUSTAINING MOTIVATION

When one starts to study a new subject there is so much to learn that it is easy to keep up interest. Progress seems relatively rapid as new discoveries are made. Unfortunately, with any subject, there comes a point at which the fundamentals have been learned, but have yet to be fully established by repetition. It is at this point that many people drop out or are unwilling to accept the facts. Work, instead of being a daily excitement, becomes a drudgery!

Of course, success provides the best motivation as there is always another goal to conquer. On the way up the ladder this is not hard, but it can be difficult to remain motivated once those goals set have been achieved. The way around this is to set new goals, and these do not necessarily have to be major. Anyone with an overriding interest in the training processes will find small things excite him, so he does not become bored. Every horse presents a new problem and there is no end to learning ways and means to overcome them. It is the absorbing interest in the training, not in the competition, that keeps a rider going; although most would admit that the incentive of the event itself drives them on.

Whatever plans are made for the future, some adjustments are bound to be necessary as each day's training is evaluated. One other point. Sitting in an armchair dreaming of success is very pleasant but, unless it is backed by action, it is likely to remain a dream!

10
The Circuit

The romantic notion that travelling all year round from one show to another is a glamorous existence, is sadly ill-founded! The truth is that it is hard work, and often exhausting and uncomfortable. Sometimes, it seems that it is one long round of packing and unpacking, with piles of damp or dirty clothes to be rushed through the washing machine and got dry ready for the next trip. Tack always seems to be filthy, needing constant cleaning, and there is usually a frantic rush to the shops for re-stocking of provisions. Horses are either being bathed or clipped, and manes and tails trimmed or plaited and, of course, all the usual household chores and urgent phone calls have to be fitted in.

Early starts with fingers freezing to the steering wheel, or arriving home at midnight after a soaking wet day are all part of 'the game'. Driving a hundred miles or so after a disappointing day can seem a very long way home!

Despite all this the keen competitor keeps going, that compulsive urge to compete being irresistible. Life for them is governed by the dressage calendar. One of the reasons for such crazy behaviour is the all-consuming hope that next time will be what you have been working for. Even when one goal is reached there is another waiting!

Rivals and Friends

To say that there is no friendship during competition would be true; in a competition it is every man for himself! Of course, this does not mean that one cannot have friends who are also competitors, but there is no room for considering how a friend will feel if you beat him. If he is a true friend he will be pleased for you, despite wishing he had won himself. Less good friends sometimes lower themselves by making detrimental remarks behind your back. These people, wishing to boost themselves, seek to undermine their rivals by making harmful remarks to judges, trainers and others. This sort of psychological warfare can be a highly successful weapon in the short term, although it seldom does any good in the long run. Experienced judges will soon see through this ploy.

Over-showing

Although people who compete cannot live without a constant rush of adrenalin, there are dangers lurking in over-showing.

The first point I want to make is especially important to the dressage purist, and that is to allow enough time for the actual training, and for ironing out problems. Being obsessed with shows can mean that training is hurried, or that the horse's mental or physical stamina is affected. A horse who loses interest in his work because it is not being done in the right way can turn sour, and if this happens it is a big problem.

Staleness may occur for several reasons. Rushing the work is one reason, since this can cause confusion and subsequent antagonism. Lack of the right conditions or fitness also may contribute, the horse becoming fed up when physically fatigued. Riding too much on hard going is another factor. Grass arenas are often responsible for this, as they can be jarring and perhaps slippery, so the horse's joints are under continual strain. Rather than go to several small competitions on grass, the wise owner will save his horse for the main event, which is more likely to be on a good artificial surface.

Many horses go stale through being continually asked to perform the same test or tests. Even if they do not start to anticipate the movements (which is likely) they can become bored and disinterested. Some end up producing a robotic, lifeless performance which is not what dressage is supposed to be about.

Over-showing also has other unwanted consequences. A judge, repeatedly seeing the same horse make mistakes week after week, will become rather fed up with seeing him! He may also become more than a little irritated if it appears that his advice is being ignored! Even if the horse starts to improve, his faults will be so well known that the judge will be looking for them.

Competing regularly means inevitably coming up against the same judges and, of course, judges discuss competitors! It is so important to gain the right reputation from the start of any career, so behaviour and presentation should be given a good deal of consideration. If it can be seen that a rider is making the right approach to his horse's training he will be gaining a head start, and will be regarded favourably.

Number and Level of Tests

So long as the horse is fit and in the right condition he could be asked to perform in one, two or even three tests on the same day at the lower levels; less in more advanced ones. This is because the latter are longer and more demanding.

There is also the question of the time allowed for riding-in which must necessarily be longer for more than one test. Compare this to the length of time the horse is exercised at home and it is easy to see how it can all be overdone. Once horse and rider are 'over the top' neither will give their best, so to ride a test then would be pointless.

Of course, if the rider has more than one horse, he may have to ride several tests, so his physical fitness is crucial. Mental alertness is also essential and to remain sufficiently primed for a long period is a hard task indeed. Each person must get to know his own capacity, so that he knows how far he can drive himself.

Riding tests of a level at which the horse has a chance of doing well is also important. It can be so fatiguing having to 'carry' the horse through his work, and the result is likely to be unsatisfactory. Also, when the rider has to make a bigger physical effort than usual, his muscles are under strain, and those that become damaged can take a long time to mend.

Travelling Distance

When beginning a show career the horse should be introduced to the whole 'scene' by being taken to small competitions quite close to home. This accustoms him to the preparation beforehand and does not tire him out.

As he progresses, the classes the rider wishes to enter will be further afield, so longer journeys are necessary. I always found journeys a strain. There is anxiety about the horse travelling well and also the hidden worries about the day ahead. The need to start out in plenty of time has already been stressed, as has the need to ensure that all necessary equipment is packed. Even so, there is always some additional point that gives pause for thought: whether to take an extra feed or haynet; ensuring there is enough fresh water aboard. Then there are the imponderables: will the temperature drop come evening, necessitating a warm rug for the journey home?

If you are fortunate enough to be competing abroad, do make sure that all the necessary paperwork is up to date, otherwise there may be infuriating hold-ups while officials check that everything is in order.

If a show is a very long distance away, or is run over more

than one day, it will be necessary to book overnight stabling. These are generally quite good but it is as well to be prepared, and a hammer and some nails do not go amiss!

Some horses settle into new surroundings very placidly, while others fret and refuse to eat. Extra titbits may help as an enticement, but if the horse loses condition the riding-in time may require some adjustment. What is very important is to make sure that the horse drinks, or is getting adequate water into his body. Feeding soaked hay may help to achieve this. Dehydration from sweating or not drinking on a long journey can have serious consequences, so do be aware of the possibility and learn about the symptoms. A dehydrated horse would certainly show severe signs of fatigue, which should prompt investigation.

Time Out

In a rider's enthusiasm to compete and 'get on', he may get so carried away that he forgets that a break from work is sometimes necessary. Horse and rider can only keep up concentrated work for so long, and young horses in particular will need a period of rest. How the owner gives his horse a holiday is an individual decision as there are several options. Also the optimum length of time may be debatable. Too long a rest and muscle has to be built up again; too short and the horse does not have time to 'let down'. The principal point, however, is that the horse will benefit and will return to his work refreshed. It is interesting to note that any exercises learned immediately prior to a rest are often recalled as if it were yesterday!

From the rider's perspective, he will also need time away from competition to consider new ideas, to ponder on past problems, or simply to forget the whole thing for a while!

Time away from competing does not always involve a holiday, however. Unless time is made for the advancement of training, the next stage cannot be reached. When organising the year ahead it is therefore essential that time is allowed between events, either for the purpose of introducing new exercises, or to consolidate old ones. Also, if things are not going as they should, the rider must be strong-minded enough to change his plans and keep the horse at home for a while.

The year is likely to be punctuated with some events more important than others. It is to these that key planning should be directed, with sufficient time allowed for adequate preparation

Surfaces

Because there can be so much variation between surfaces the competitor is constantly presented with a different 'feel'. Obtaining the right 'feel' is the basis upon which a rider relies, so it can be very worrying when it alters, as he is not sure whether the change is caused by him, the horse, or the arena.

Hard surfaces are unpleasant to work on. Not only are they jarring for the rider, they can take a toll on the horse too. On the other hand, too soft or heavy a surface will drag the horse down and make the work extremely difficult. Getting it right is not easy, but modern manufacturers have done a good job in producing synthetic surfaces that are pleasant to ride on. (Affording them is another matter, and some people have to train at home on one type and compete at a show on another; never an easy task!)

Of the natural substances, it is my opinion that bark should be avoided. Once wet it becomes very slippery, and this can destroy the confidence of both horse and rider. Sand is heavy but safe, and if mixed with sawdust can be quite a good surface. If it is too deep it will shift about, adversely affecting the horse's gaits.

Riding on grass has already been mentioned as unsuitable for the serious competitor. Any ground likely to become poached will cause irregularities in the gaits and loss of balance. Any surface which inhibits the rider from being able to make the horse work will, of course, seriously hold up training.

While indoor surfaces have the advantage of not being affected by weather, they do have their own problems. Unless they are adequately watered, dust will be a health hazard. Also, unless watering is done carefully, some areas will hold water while others remain dry. This can be dangerous if it causes the horse to slip.

Only by practising on a variety of surfaces will a rider gain a true picture of the difficulties involved. This will be particularly applicable when trying to set up a musical kür as timing can alter drastically if the surface at the competition is very different from the one at home. Although there is no easy answer to this it is important to be aware of the problem so that thought can at least be given to it.

Accepting Limitations

Regular competitors on the 'circuit' will find that they inevitably meet up with the same combinations time and again. This does mean that an 'order' becomes almost established, with certain names appearing in the frame on a regular basis. Although good training is the basis of success it must be said, and accepted, that those horses with good training *and* star quality will come out on top. Those who do not have horses quite in this league may find this depressing, becoming fed up when the 'top slot' eludes them. Unfortunately, it is necessary to be realistic and accept that with some animals the 'top slot' may never be achievable.

Being ruthless enough to part with a horse you have trained, who is also a friend, is very hard indeed and some people just cannot do it. In this case, striving for top honours may simply be unrealistic. There are also plenty of horses who are generally good at the job but find one specific exercise particularly difficult. It could be well worth keeping such a horse as, despite this handicap, he may well win more than he loses. He will undoubtedly give his rider useful experience even though he may never become exceptional.

In dressage it is so important that the 'picture' is right and if judges repeatedly say it is not, it is useless to fight the inevitable. Of course, no-one should give up too easily. A thorough investigation into all problems is essential. Many can be surmounted, and parting with a horse should be a last resort.

Conclusion

Being a competitive person undeniably means having a desire to win. Actually to succeed means also having the will.

Desire on its own sometimes clouds the fundamental factors necessary to fulfil that desire – which in the case of dressage are the enhancement of the horse's natural abilities and the gaining of his full co-operation.

With a strong will the sacrifices necessary, the personal discipline and the commitment are more readily accepted. At times of uncertainty it is the mental approach, the essential determination of the mind to dominate the outcome, that will make the difference. With this awareness I am confident that the truly committed will go forwards to victory.